Life Is for the Living

A COLLECTION OF ESSAYS AND STORIES ON LIFE AND LIVING

Dr. Edward A. Moses MD

Contents

About the Author

Edward A. Moses is a retired physician who was born in Trinidad, West Indies in 1933, of Syrian Parents. He is at present residing in Florida, USA with his wife of more than fifty years. They have four children.

He received his medical training at the University of Sheffield, England, and returned to practice in Trinidad. In 1967 he returned to England to pursue post-graduate training in Psychiatry and upon completion he returned to Trinidad where he was appointed consultant in charge of the Psychiatric unit at the General Hospital. He also continued a successful private practice in family medicine and psychiatry.

In addition to his extensive medical duties, he was very involved in a variety of medical, governmental, social and philanthropic activities in Trinidad and Tobago. These involved such diverse fields as school and prison reform, drug abuse, mental health, Red Cross activities and public education. In 1976 he was awarded the Medal of Merit (Gold) by the Government of Trinidad and Tobago for Public Services.

He travelled extensively to countries in North and South America and to Europe, mainly on official business.

In 1980, as a result unexpected circumstances, including the very serious illness of his son, he moved to Florida where he initially joined the Department of Family Practice and then subsequently went out into private practice in Coral Springs, Florida. He spent the next 30 years in this practice until he retired in 2010.

He has continued to be actively involved in social affairs in Trinidad and locally. He spends a lot of time pursuing his dual interests of collecting quotations and writing essays on all aspects of life and living.

Foreword

> *"Life is but a walking Shadow, a poor Player That*
> *Struts and frets his Hour upon the Stage,*
> *And then is heard no more;*
> *It is a tall tale, told by an Idiot,*
> *full of Sound and Fury, signifying nothing."*

*I*f we accepted this description of Life offered by *William Shakespeare* in one of his greatest tragedies, *Macbeth*, then life loses all its meaning and we are reduced to a pathetic, sorry state where, as so many Nihilistic people believe, we are born, we live and then die without any reason or any purpose.

I completely reject this position. To me life is not meant to be a random series of transient, overlapping and unrelated experiences which once completed are destined to be consigned to oblivion. I believe instead, life is an exquisite and precious expression of a greater plan by a Supreme Being in which our time spent on earth is but a short segment of a journey which began in eternity and will continue into eternity. I believe further, that while we are on this journey we will encounter a series of experiences, many real and others fictional or imaginary which serve to mold us into the persons who we are.

To me the real essence, or more accurately, the paradox of life is what determines where and how we choose to travel on the journey. While we have been granted this special privilege to participate on this journey, we are under no direct influence to follow fixed rules, but rather we have been given total freedom of will to express our lives as we choose. Because of this we, as human beings, unlike the animals of the world who are committed to a life totally dictated by instinct and by need, are free to make and change choices as we see fit. This has clear advantages but at the same time carry serious consequences, as we travel along.

When we begin the journey at birth, we do not have any control over the road or direction to choose. This is done by our parents or guardians. However as we develop, we acquire the ability to modify the road we choose and the direction we travel, giving us free choice for how far we may travel. This I believe does not occur as others have suggested, as a result of random selection or mere chance, but as part of an organized and orderly plan by a Supreme Being.

Albert Einstein, the great physicist and humanist, expressed these sentiments in the following terms:

> *"I don't try to imagine a God. It suffices to stand in awe of the structure of the world, insofar as it allows our inadequate senses to appreciate it."*

He explained his belief further by stating unequivocally, that there was a purpose and intent in life and it was up to us to search out the true meaning and to fulfill it to the best of our ability.

From the onset, everyone is afforded several options from which to choose the ultimate path to travel on. Some choose the easier path of going along with the crowd and sharing in the benefits or paying the price of this action. Others reject this easy way and adopt their own direction and make their own choices. To me, this indeed is the original intent of the Almighty. By granting us the freedom to do as we please, we have the opportunity to find out about ourselves, to select from several options and above all, to avail ourselves of the opportunity to learn from our experiences or from those of others before us. In this way we will have no excuses to offer when the final judgment is upon us and we have arrived at the end of the road. It is left entirely up to us to make use of the many opportunities and landmarks that lay strewn along the road we travel. Whether they result from our personal experiences or from those of others who have gone before us, they are available for us to use them as lessons on our own journey.

I see these landmarks as essential threads that make up the whole fabric of our life as we know and experience it. Because of them, I see all that we do, and all that we experience, and all that has been told to us, and all that has been recorded not standing in isolation of one from the other to be viewed as separate and unrelated entities. Rather they must be viewed as interrelated and interconnected in much the same way as the stones that lay scattered along the road of life. They form a unique mosaic pattern that is peculiarly our own and as a result they are an integral part of our fabric of life and cannot be ignored. They occupy our thoughts, our actions and our life.

With this in mind, in this book I propose to briefly deal with a multitude of aspects of life as I have encountered them either personally, or from other sources, along the way. The topics chosen are presented without any chronological order. They are, however, grouped under general headings dealing with subjects of similar affinity. I was guided mainly by a desire to share my thoughts and my feelings on my life as I see them. They were not chosen to influence the reader in any way, nor are they meant to be a guide to be followed. Rather they are meant to be a reference that readers can use as they see fit. I will also include quotations from time to time specially selected for each topic because of their impact upon me, and for no other reason.

If this serves to initiate interest, thought or discussion by the reader then I consider my efforts fully rewarded.

Edward A. Moses, MD

Acknowledgments

*F*or as long as I can remember I have been in love with quotations. I remember the first time I took note of a quotation was one that was painted on the wall of the local Society for the Poor. I was no more that 10 years old and it read:

> *"No one is useless in this world*
> *who lightens the burdens of another."*

I found out later that it was recorded by Charles Dickens in one of his short stories entitled "Dr. Marigold". I have never forgotten that encounter not only because it was the first book of my own choice I read, but it also set me off on a life-long quest for meaningful quotations that after more than four score years is yet to abate.

This effort however has come out of the encouragement of my four children and others to compile and record selected essays from my collection so that I could leave them with a record that says something of me after I have passed on. That makes sense to me because nothing I leave behind speaks so much of me as the essays.

I want to thank most especially my cousin Joe Sabga who never gave up trying to persuade me to complete the task. I also acknowledge my Son Ted, my Niece Natalya and especially my Nephew Chris for spending so much time helping in all aspects of this endeavor. If this ever comes to completion I certainly acknowledge its success to the selfless efforts of all these young people.

But above all I want to express my sincerest gratitude to my wife Gloria who from the beginning was a constant supporter and my most loyal fan. And to my children, Sylvia, Sarah, Sonya and Ted whose unwavering confidence and subtle encouragement ensured my continued application, even after I had returned home from that severe illness in April, 2014.

To all of them I dedicate this effort.

Edward A. Moses, MD

Introduction

Life is a journey of learning available to all who have been granted the opportunity to travel.

You may choose to accept the opportunities offered and grow in stature.

or –

You may choose not to do so and drift along in blissful ignorance.

Life's Lessons

As we travel along the road of Life we come in contact with a large and varied mix of people, situations and experiences. Most of these, like passing clouds, will impact us for a fleeting moment and then move on, leaving little or no memory or imprint.

However, from time to time, someone, or something or some experience occurs and so affects us, that from then on our lives are changed permanently and irreversibly. We can all relate to the thousands of such occurrences that have taken place in our personal lives and recall the impact of each one on us. Often they remain permanently visible like so many milestones scattered along the way, but on other occasions they are buried into our psyche only to appear on special occasions.

In my own life, as I am sure with every one else, there have been very many examples of people whose influence and advice on me easily come to mind. Some of them stand out like beacons indelibly imprinted and deeply embedded in my psyche. I can think of My Parents, who by word and by example taught me the meaning of honesty, loyalty and family commitment. My late Uncle, from whom I gratefully acknowledge the true meaning of honor, responsibility and justice and to Rev. Fr. Graf, my High School Science teacher, who instilled the love of learning and of sacrifice into my young, impressionable mind. Even now, having crossed my 80th year, I still recall these experiences gratefully and fondly, and try always to pass on the lessons learnt to succeeding generations.

Brett Favre, the hall-of-fame quarterback who led the Green Bay Packers successfully for several years, has been quoted as follows:

> *"Life deals you a lot of Lessons;*
> *Some people learn from them, some people don't."*

This simple statement crystallizes in a few words the real meaning of the lessons of life. As we proceed along the road of life we are all constantly exposed to opportunities to learn and grow in knowledge and insight. Lessons are all around us and opportunities surface in every aspect of our lives. How we meet them and how we make use of them makes the difference.

Most people blunder through life expecting that everything will be done for them and unwilling to expend energy or effort toward their growth and improvement. What a pity, for they end up living out their lives in blissful ignorance, cheated from the rewards awaiting them if only they would help themselves. Others welcome the opportunities, irrespective of difficulty, as valuable chances to learn more and be more. These are the people who will benefit from all of life's blessings. They are the leaders, the innovators, the inventors, the thinkers and all the other successful people to whom the rest of us look with awe and admiration.

Abigail Adams, the wife of John Adams, the second president of the United States, in one of her essays wrote:

> *"Learning is not attained by chance;*
> *It must be sought for with ardor and attended to with diligence"*

Perhaps we can learn from this advice, and be more alert and diligent to the lessons of life as we continue our travels along the road.

> *There are no mistakes or failures;*
> *-Only Lessons*
> *.......Denis Waitley*

The greatest Lesson in life;
is to know that even fools can sometimes be right
........Horace

He who follows his Lessons tastes a profound peace.
.......Moliere

Lessons are not given, they are taken.
........Cesare Pavese

Family Ties

The Family is the most fundamental part of Human existence. It is made up not only of Fathers and Mothers, Brothers and Sisters and Aunts and Uncles and all others descended from common ancestors.

But it can also include others as well who, through union, association or common beliefs and shared interests, occupy a position of trust and kinship.

These all form a special unit and reflect a closeness based on true respect and caring. Regardless of what may happen to others, a true family provides a safe harbor where every member can find safety and support in good times and bad times.

Life as the Lighthouse
(A Father's Role)

"You represent that Lighthouse to me, because no matter how stormy the seas of life became, you were always that pillar, the beacon of light to guide me through the trying times.
No matter how rough or dark things may seem, your strength and your unmistakable guiding light brought me to a sound conclusion."

These words, written by my son Ted on the occasion of my 75th birthday, touched me more than anything else I heard that night or since. I can think of nothing that so completely describes the role of a successful father as he performs his sacred duties of guiding his child through the storms of life.

A lighthouse is a structure placed by the maker to guide and protect its people as they navigate through life's treacherous and stormy waters. To provide the necessary light and signals by word, by action and by example to bring them into safe harbors. To be successful, it must stand as a monument to motivation, and be consistent and unwavering in its standards. To be effective, it must remain tall and strong, and must be able to withstand the pounding of the waves, the onslaught of the rain and the terror of lightning and thunder, all the while its tireless beacon showing the way without change or interruption.

As I see it, a father's role is no different and no less sacred from that of a lighthouse. He must first recognize that his children are sacred responsibilities merely entrusted to him for care and guidance, as *Khalil Gibran* so beautifully described:

"Your children are not your children.
They are the sons and daughters of Life's longing for itself.
They came through you, but not from you, and though they are with
you, yet they belong not to you."

Like the Lighthouse, a father must be committed to provide the guiding light to help them navigate through the troubled and daunting road to maturity with fairness and consistency. The way each person sees the world depends on the experiences and lessons acquired on their journey through life, and like the lighthouse, their success or failure is directly related to the omnipresent structure with its guiding light shining over every character and every action. This is the true role of the father.

Nothing is more unsettling than to encounter fathers whose selfish motivation drive them to compete with, rather than guide their child. Or worse still, the absent father whose callous, wanton abandonment of his responsibility makes him worse than an animal. They all hide behind such statements as *"my father never helped me and I did very well"*. This is very unfortunate and to my mind, very unacceptable. There can be no excuse for abandonment of responsibility except in illness or death. Even when, for whatever reason the parents separate, there can be no excuse for the Father to relinquish his sacred role.

As I see it, the role of a true father is that of being present to provide guidance and direction without control or domination. And in the same manner he must provide the necessary tools and opportunities to help the child develop to its full potential. *Clarence B. Kellard*, the prolific American author recorded this observation in one of his essays in eloquent simplicity:

"My Father didn't tell me how to live;
He lived, and let me watch him do it."

There is an indescribable honor and pride in every father who is blessed with children in whom he is able to reap the reward of his efforts. No amount of material wealth or personal possessions can match the feeling of a proud father, or for that matter, replace the desolation and disappointment of disenchanted children. In this context, like all very successful lighthouses, there has to be constant attention paid to maintaining the highest levels of performance and a willingness to adapt and adjust to the prevailing changes. A father's biggest mistake is to continue to take things for granted and not recognize that as circumstances change, so do needs and expectations. He needs to know every day that to be worthy of the respect of his children, demands eternal vigilance and flexibility.

For myself, I often recall a prayer written by an unknown author to constantly remind me of this noble responsibility. I strongly recommend it to all true fathers:

"One night a father overheard his son pray:
'Dear God, make me the kind of man my Dad is.'
Later that night, the father prayed:
"Dear God, make me the kind of man my son wants me to be."

And you Fathers do not provoke your children to wrath;
Bring them up in the training and admonition of the Lord.
…..Ephesians 6:4

A Father's words are like a thermostat;
That sets the temperature in the house.
…..Paul Lewis

Good Fathers make good sons.
….Author Unknown

I cannot think of any need in childhood as strong,
as the need for a Father's protection.
….Sigmund Freud

It is a wise Father, who knows his child.
….William Shakespeare

It is much easier to become a Father, than to be one.
…..Kent Nerburn

When you teach your son, you teach your son's son.
…..The Talmud

I talk, and talk, and I haven't taught people in 50 years
what my father taught by example in one week."
……..Mario Cuomo

Life with Today's Mother

As children we would often ask our late mother which of the seven of us is her favorite one?

She would invariably answer by reciting this old Arab proverb:

> *"My favorite child is:*
> *The baby, until he grows up;*
> *The one who is sick, until he gets better;*
> *The one who is away, until he comes home;*
> *The one who is worried, until he stops worrying;*
> *And then all my children, for as long as I live."*

Historically, a good mother was expected to devote her whole life to her family. She was the glue that held the family together, that provided loving and supporting care, and ensured the stable and consistent environment needed by the growing child. Above all else, the nurturing provided by a mother plays a vital and irreplaceable role in the growth and development of a child. She was the care-giver, the nurse, the provider, the teacher, the advisor and the protector wrapped up in a single package. She felt obligated to care for the family and put their needs before all else, willingly setting aside personal aspirations however urgent, without hesitation. The effect of her role was beautifully described by the following quotation taken from the pages of the *Godey's Lady's Book, 1867,* a popular 19th century publication, with which we can all identify:

"About every true mother there is sanctity of martyrdom-
and when she is no more in the body, her children see her with the ring
of light around her head."

Over the last several decades women's roles have changed significantly and as a result certain facts related to the priority of choices have also changed. This includes society's present vision of a woman as a multifaceted creature; one that should be able to manage professional and personal aspirations with equal success and finesse as she copes with her maternal responsibilities. In our current society many problems arise from these complex roles of the new mother, and traditional beliefs are being tested as never before. With the increasing role of the mother as a second (and sometimes first) bread-winner, the increasing breakdown of the conventional family unit, and the rising tendency to single parent household, it is becoming extremely difficult for mothers to provide everything a child needs to ensure optimum growth. Not only must they provide the care and support a child needs, but they must also provide enough income for the family to live on. Even with the best intentions and increased effort, this situation frequently leads to problems within the family. Some of which could have a negative effect on the children and compromise normal growth and development.

It takes learning and practice to become a qualified mother. It is not an easy job because future mothers must learn by example and experience as they go. It is much better if they were raised in a caring home by a caring parent fully committed to pass it on to the child. Unfortunately in today's setting with her increased demands, the mother is not able to devote the time and attention to the children. The result is that she is not able to truly pass on the "old fashioned" maternal skills in the way that her mother was able to do. This has led to succeeding generations of young women with less of the skills of their predecessors and less inclination to follow their examples. When this is added to the increasing demand for self sufficiency and work opportunity, it is not difficult to visualize the changing image of modern motherhood, with increasing use of adjunct help like nurseries, pre-school and babysitters to augment the mother's role.

I make no excuse in lamenting the progressive demise of the full time, stay-at-home mother with all the irreplaceable advantages it carries for the successful care, support and growth of the family. Equally, I do not deny that even in this modern day of the multifaceted mother, there are many instances of exceptional work done by these mothers and their children have grown healthy and mature. The difference is that it is so much more difficult to ensure optimum results with the latter's approach.

In the end, no one will deny the unique and special place held by the mother in every society and in every family unit. It is one that must never be compromised for any reason or excuse whatsoever. I can do no better than to repeat the words of *Washington Irving*, the great 19th century American author and historian, in his own sensitive and special way, describing his view of *a* Mother:

"A Mother is the truest friend we have.
When trials, heavy and sudden, fall upon us,
When adversity takes the place of prosperity,
When friends who rejoice with us in our sunshine
But desert us when troubles thicken around us,
Still will she cling to us, and endeavor by her kind precepts
and counsels, to dissipate the clouds of darkness,
and cause peace to return to our hearts."

The hand that rocks the cradle is the hand that rules the world.
. . . . . . .W. R. Wallace

A man loves his Sweetheart the most, his Wife the best,
- - - - - - -but his Mother the longest.
. . . .Irish Proverb

God could not be everywhere and therefore he made mothers.
. . . . . .Rudyard Kipling

All that I am or ever hope to be, I owe to my Angel Mother.
.........Abraham Lincoln

The most important thing a father can do for his children,
is to love their Mother.
.....Author Unknown

A mother is not a person to lean on,
but a person to make leaning unnecessary.
.... Dorothy Canfield Fisher

Mother is the name for God in the lips and hearts of all little children
........William Makepeace Thakeray

Life as my Brother's Keeper

> *"And love will hold us together*
> *Make us a shelter to weather the storm.*
> *And I'll be my brother's keeper*
> *so the whole world would know that we're not alone."*

*T*he above quotation is taken from a song entitled *Hold us together,* written and performed by *Matthew Maher,* a critically acclaimed Canadian-born contemporary religious singer, songwriter and record artist. It draws attention to the question that has been asked over and over throughout the ages. A question that has plagued humanity since its original record in the biblical story, when Cain murdered his brother Abel in a jealous rage and then replied to God's enquiry:

> *"I don't know. Am I my brother's keeper?"*

The term *"brother's keeper",* especially in the Judeo-Christian traditions, has come to symbolize the willingness to accept the welfare of your fellow man and the unconditional responsibility to exercise the necessary choices. In its truest sense it implies a moral obligation and a directive as children of God, to care for your brother. Jesus Christ, in teaching us the prayer to God, began with *"Our Father who art in heaven."* This clearly alluded that as children of God we accept the brotherhood of mankind and therefore our individual responsibility to one another. St. Paul in his *letter to the Galatians, Chapter 3, Verse 28* was more direct and unambiguous when he wrote:

"There is neither Jew nor Greek, there is neither bond nor free.
There is neither male nor female; for ye are all one in Christ Jesus."

And when Jesus, in *Matthew Chapter 22, Verse 39*, instructed us to *"Love your neighbor as yourself"*, he was confirming the principle of responsibility for the caring of one another.

Unfortunately, the real tragedy and the failure of humanity throughout the ages is that, although we have always given lip service to this concept, we have never, as individuals or as groups, or as a society or as a nation, seriously acknowledged its relevance. Except for the occasional individual, who by example and by life choice, has attempted to fulfill this directive, we have chosen to place our selfish needs ahead of all else, securing our own comforts at all cost. We will very seldom admit to the fact, but the truth is abundantly clear, that in all things, we do everything in our power to secure our own welfare and more, while giving little attention to our neighbors' needs. Without question, we are motivated by our in-bred animal instinct which dictates a *"Me First"* response.

Over the years, the world has seen many examples of people who voluntarily abandoned a life of potential glory and success to follow the advice of Christ and become their brother's keeper. My personal favorite is *Dr. Albert Schweitzer*, a German theologian, an accomplished world class organist, philosopher and physician. He forsook a life of fame and recognition in Europe, to become a medical missionary to the inhabitants of *Lambarene*, a small outpost in French Equatorial Africa, founding and maintaining a hospital to serve the population. He was motivated by an ethical philosophy of sharing, which he called *"Reverence For Life"*, for which he received a *Nobel Peace Prize* in 1952. Despite the multitude of accolades and awards he received from all over the world, Schweitzer, who died and is buried in Lambarene, in 1965, remained dedicated to his principle of reverence and responsibility to life.

But Schweitzer is but one outstanding example of many, many others who on a daily basis spend their lives guided by the principle of caring for the welfare of others. Each day, in thousands of ways and often at great personal expense and inconvenience, people can be found going the extra mile in order in some small way, to alleviate the pain and suffering of others. Consider these events;

a very successful and prominent Neurosurgeon leaves his comfortable offices in Miami to travel and spend weeks at a time in Haiti under appalling conditions after a devastating earthquake, or a fireman goes into a burning building to save a victim, or a 16 year old student saves her weekly allowance to send to a children's fund. These are all examples of living as your brother's keeper. Consider the example of Mary, a kind lady who has suffered her share of misfortunes. She lost her only son at 31 and shortly after was fired from her cleaning job by an ignorant boss. Yet with no source of income but charity from her friends she continues to collect clothes and food to give to her needy brothers and sisters in her neighborhood.

All these people, in their own special way, were indeed living the life proscribed by Jesus Christ in the Gospel of Matthew when he said:

> *"Whatever you do to the least of my brothers,*
> *You do to me"*

The image and kindness of these people, quietly doing their work without pomp and glory, stands out in stark and glaring contrast when compared with so many of the "famous" people whose names and faces inhabit the daily newspapers, the weekly magazines and the nightly television programs and whose claim to fame is the absurd and immoral exploitation of self gratification. A young woman who is said to have collected 15 million dollars to participate in a public marriage ceremony and then breaks it up after 90 days, or the investor who knowingly cheated and schemed thousands of people out of their life savings, with no intention of repayment, or the college coach who used his position and trust to abuse young children are but a few examples of what appears to be the norm in present-day society.

By any standard, in any society, these actions are both a gross abomination and shameful indictment of ungodly behavior. Yet society is determined to glorify and reward these people to absurd levels and we, as members of society, encourage this transgression by our support or even worse, by our silence. It makes the true believer feel that Jesus Christ suffered and died in vain and that his teachings of love and caring remain buried in the mud of selfishness.

But irrespective of the prevailing conditions around us, it is essential that we all make the effort to embrace the spirit of respect, caring and tolerance towards our neighbors and to recognize that we are indeed our brother's keepers. Without this principle firmly implanted, we are destined to continue to live in a world of suffering, turmoil and distrust. In the setting as presently exists, dominated by wars, racial and religious distrust, indiscriminate killing and absurd social imbalances, it is no surprise that Schweitzer's principle of *Reverence of Life* has been discarded on the altar of expediency. The task is not easy, but not impossible, and must begin with the acceptance and recognition of the fact that each one of us are indeed keepers and instead of asking, we rise up and accept the responsibility with diligence and determination.

Many years ago, during a very trying time in my life, I found myself in need of others to help me deal with a difficult personal situation. I was sustained not only by the selfless support of others but by the words of a beautiful song, recorded by *"The Hollies"* entitled *"He Ain't Heavy."* They have since served to constantly remind me of the need, role and strength of being a keeper. I sincerely hope they will serve the same purpose for you:

> *"It's a long, long road from which there is no return.*
> *While we're on our way to there, why not share?*
> *And the load doesn't weigh me down at all.*
> *He ain't heavy, he's my brother."*

> *We are commanded to seek out those who are lost.*
> *We are to be our brother's keeper*
> *…..Joseph B. Wirthlin.*
> *(American businessman and church leader)*

Sisters and Brothers

*A*s the youngest boy in a family of seven with only one younger sister, I have always felt that the strongest link in my life is the support of my siblings. We were brought up by parents whose commitment to the welfare and success of their children stood above all else and who passed onto us a strong sense of family unity and commitment. These feelings have never faltered even after the passage of many decades.

Whenever I reflect on the meaning of my family to me, I invariably recall the unforgettable words ascribed to Clara Ortega:

> *"To the outside world we all grow old, but not to brothers and sisters.*
> *We know each other as we always were, we know each other's hearts.*
> *We share private family jokes. We remember family feuds and secrets,*
> *family grieves and joys. We live outside the touch of time".*

Although time and circumstances have a way of moving us forward and away from the secure world of childhood and of changing us into the people we are today with separate needs, priorities, responsibilities and commitments, the invisible bond remains strong and continuous. *—And so they should be!*

And as our individual lives become more involved and more complex, we inevitably drift further away into our own individual world, building our own families and our own separate identities. But yet throughout this journey wherever we travel, we are but one word, one thought away. We are ready to drop all to support the one when the call comes. When our eldest brother succumbed to cancer we came together to mourn his untimely loss and to support each other. When our eldest sister departed, despite all else including serious internal family conflict, we came together to share in the loss. And when another sister succumbed to the ravages of Alzheimers' disease, the rest of us suffered the loss together.

Now, even as the ravages of time bear down upon each of us taking its toll of each one in its own way, we worry and we pray that God, in his kindness, will continue to protect us and allow us the time to share our memories and to enjoy one another for a while longer.

Even after the passage of time, we each continue to deal with our loss in different ways. Some have become stronger and others continue to carry regrets, but we are all united in acceptance. Knowing deep in our heart that one day we will again come together and share the love and commitment so lovingly passed on by our parents. Equally, in times of celebrations and good fortune, we look forward to sharing the joy and happiness with all, and remain unhappy and unfulfilled unless we are able to come together and share our good feelings with one another. It feels so natural that the joy of one is shared by all, equally. This is simply because that's the way it should be among brothers and sisters.

And even as we grow older and travel further apart along the road of life, our concerns for one another, and each others' welfare grows more acute. The news of the illness of one sibling creates an urgency among the others until resolution occurs. This is an inevitable consequence of the bond within us and a desire to keep it intact for as long as we can. For if I have learnt anything from the example of our late parents is that the Family is Paramount and stands above all else. And rest assured I intend to pass this lesson on to my own children and then, God willing, to their children.

You don't choose your family.
They are God's gift to you, as you are to them.
......Bishop Desmond Tutu

Other things may change us, but we start and end with Family.
.......Anthony Brandt

The happiest moments of my life have been the few which
I have passed at home in the bosom of my family.
........Thomas Jefferson

Families are the compasses that guide us.
They are the inspiration to reach great heights,
and our comfort when we occasionally falter.
.......Brad Henry

Brothers and sisters are as close as hands and feet.
....Vietnamese Proverb

There's no other love like the love for a brother.
...Astrid Alauda

Life with Neighbors

"*Far better a Neighbor near you,
than a brother who is far off.*"

I was recently reminded by my brother-in-law of this quotation contained in *Proverbs 27:10*, during a discussion on the subject of relationships with neighbors. He was lamenting the fact that unlike past times, there was a growing tendency to keep away from our neighbors in the name of increased privacy and of avoiding giving the impression of being inquisitive. He added that in years gone by a good neighbor was considered to be a blessing that deserves respect and honor. Further, he added that the definition of neighbor should extend not only to the person next door but should include residents of up to 40 houses in all directions. In effect, this really includes the whole neighborhood.

By definition a neighbor is someone who lives in close proximity to you and with whom you share common boundary. But in truth this is a relative term which depends on a number of variables relating to whether you are a city dweller, an urban dweller or a rural dweller. It should not necessarily be restricted to the immediate contact but to any one with whom a relationship is developed. A good neighbor is one who is friendly, caring and considerate, who respects your space and privacy but who is always ready and willing to extend support and help whenever it is needed. He is one who takes time to reach out and connect, to talk and smile, to look out for the welfare of your children and your property and above all, do nothing to initiate or encourage any ill-will. In fact a good neighbor is the most essential component for a successful community, and no community will ever survive without the help of good neighbors.

In my own experience, in my many years of living in various countries and different cultures, I have been blessed on all but one occasion, with good neighbors with whom I have shared many rewarding relationships. We have shared happiness and sorrows, success and failures, good news and bad news, all the time respecting one another's need for privacy and discretion. Indeed I feel very comfortable in saying that a good neighbor is as important as any member of my family and deserves as much respect. There was however, one occasion where I had the great misfortune of living next to a neighbor who chose to exercise his right to complete privacy and isolation. The environment was at best regrettable. In my mind, it certainly confirmed the statement "*better an enemy than a bad neighbor*". For with an enemy, you are always prepared to protect yourself, but with such a neighbor, I was overwhelmed with a sense of ambivalence and uncertainty.

But neighbors are not only individuals who share adjoining spaces. They are also communities and countries sharing common boundaries. As in the case of individual neighbors, they also are bound by the same rules of mutual respect and responsibility which if applied, will lead to mutual peace and prosperity for all. Unfortunately this is not the case in so many situations. The world is in a state of such intense turmoil and conflict for reasons based more on selfish desires to conquer and control than any legitimate excuse. This has resulted in the infliction of such unimaginable pain and suffering on so many defenseless people, whose only need is to live in peace and safety. We need only to examine any of the conflicts which have caused, and continue to cause, such severe economic and personal suffering, to really see that the root cause is the product of a few, misguided, misinformed and biased individuals who, like bad neighbors, are prepared to cause untold conflict and misery, to satisfy their own agenda. The classic among these is the long running conflict between the Arabs of Palestine and the Jews of Israel. They share the lands, the waters and food supply but are kept apart by religious and political fears.

These people, whether they are your next door neighbor, or the president of a country waging war against a neighboring country, or the leader of a religious group condemning another religious group or any other similar conflict, invariably justify their actions by invoking the name of the Almighty who they

insist is on their side. What a crying shame that they do so, for were they genuinely concerned with the wishes of the Almighty God they will no doubt be
aware of his own words as related to us in *Luke Chapter 10, Verse 27:*

> *"You shall love your God with all your heart,*
> *And with all your soul, and with all your strength,*
> *And with all your mind:*
> *-And love your neighbor as your self."*

> *He who sleeps contently, while his neighbors sleep hungry,*
> *Did not believe my message.*
> *.....Prophet Mohammad*

> *Great Spirit, grant that I may not criticize my neighbor;*
> *Until I have walked a mile in his moccasins.*
> *...... American Indian Prayer.*

> *You can fool the devil,*
> *but you can't fool the Neighbors.*
> *......Francis Bacon*

> *When strangers start acting like Neighbors;*
> *....Communities are reinvigorated.*
> *......Ralph Nader*

> *Don't throw stones at your Neighbors;*
> *-Especially if your own windows are glass.*
> *.....Benjamin Franklin*

> *Few of us could bear to have ourselves as Neighbors.*
> *......Mignon McLaughlin*

A man is called selfish not for pursuing his own good,
but for neglecting his Neighbor's.
. . . . . . .Richard Whately

A Young Man's Dilemma
A Short Story of Despair and Loss

*S*ome years ago I returned to the UK to my old Alma Mater to spend six months doing a brief refresher course. During my stay I unfortunately was informed of a tragic episode which had occurred to a patient of a colleague of mine.

My colleague and I had completed our studies together and while I returned home to continue my career, he elected to stay back and had not left the area since. He settled in a small community just outside the city with his wife and family and had in fact done very well for himself. He related the story which had occurred about 1 month earlier and which had left this small community badly shaken, looking for answers. It affected me then, and has continued to affect me ever since, because of the fact that it continues to occur in communities all over the world and no one seems to be willing to expend the genuine effort necessary to stop it. This is the story as I recall it:

The early sun came in through the window in all its glory as William opened his eyes. He looked at the clock next to his bed, and then instinctively looked over to see if James was still sleeping. It was only six o'clock and it was Saturday. Why the hell was he up so damn early on the one day he does not have to get ready for school he thought, but the strange feeling he felt within him quickly answered his concern. James was not in the bed. This worried him a great deal because he knew his elder brother was always a late sleeper and in fact seldom ever wakes up without vigorous urging from him or his mother. He was only 11 years old but he felt like 40 years as this strange, cold/hot/burning feeling sailed over him. Something was wrong!

He jumped out of the bed and headed to the Living Room but James was not there! He quickly set about to find him. With each passing minute he felt more and more that something was going very wrong. That lump in his throat was getting bigger and bigger. He headed to the play room, and then the study room and then the garage but there was no sign of James. He even checked to see if his bicycle was gone, but it was most present. "Oh God!" he thought "I'm scared" but he did not understand why he felt like this, as he roamed from room to room. Finally as he entered the basement he saw it! A sight that he knew will haunt him and everyone else in the house, for eternity and beyond. There he was, a belt around his neck securely attached to a support bar, eyes wide open and both hand grabbing on to it as if he attempted to release it. He had died without saying anything to anyone. Without giving any indication that he had planned this or even thought about it. He was gone forever and Willy was left alone!

The outpouring of genuine shock and affection was unbelievable. His family was distraught. His parents, as one would expect were overwhelmed with sorrow and pain. The community at large lamented this senseless loss and the media overflowed with editorials, letters and opinions expressing this grave trend in our society. The home was inundated, night after night, by scores of his fellow students and friends, and even strangers, who started nightly meetings, complete with prayers and testimonials to the deceased. Some even went so far as to call these nightly sessions a vigil.

No one really knew the real reason for this catastrophic action taken by James. Even my colleague, who has known the family both socially and professionally for years, did not anticipate this turn of event. He, like so many others could only surmise as to what might have happened. The truth will never be known since it died with the only person who really knew it. On the surface he appeared to have everything going for him. As a student, his academic achievements consistently placed him in the upper 10% of his class and he was considered to be a very good University prospect. He was an excellent debater and led his school to many successful efforts as its captain. He excelled in rugby and was considered to be the best hooker the school had ever had, helping it to reach the area finals. Overall he was certainly one of the most popular and well known members of his form six year and was being seriously considered as a worthy candidate for next year's school prefect. He was never ever depressed and no one ever saw an angry outburst from him. As the Principal himself remarked in his eulogy at the funeral; *"He was the last person I would ever have thought would think of, far less carry out, this heinous action."*

Tragically, it would appear in retrospect that this is far from the truth. James was in fact a victim of circumstances for which he had no control. They appeared to be so heavily stacked up against him that, except for a supernatural intervention or overwhelming good luck, he was destined to suffer a catastrophic outcome. And this is not, by any means a unique occurrence. For as long as recorded history has existed, there have been stories written about people who have suffered disastrous consequences at the hands of destiny and circumstances beyond their control. Throughout the ages, the literature of all the ancient cultures is overflowing with stories of similar tragedies. The ancient Chinese philosophers, the Greek and Roman authors such as Aristotle, Euripides and Seneca and the great Renaissance poets as exemplified by William Shakespeare spent a large part of their literary efforts recording these episodes. This young man was indeed a tragedy of his time, no different than Hamlet or Romeo and Juliet in their time and like them, the outcome was inevitable and tragic.

James was the first born of two young people who spent their early lives in a rebellious mode. They were each talented and headstrong, and preferred to reject conformity. From an early age they both were sources of much parental concern, school complaints and social maladjustments, without regard to the consequences. Despite this, James's father possessed a very likable personality and was quite shrewd, and as a result, despite his continued habits, he became a very successful salesman and was able to earn a very comfortable living. His mother, though not completing her education, showed outstanding natural ability which gained her much respect. Paradoxically however, despite or perhaps as a result of their rebellious past, they became very rigid, unyielding parents with their two sons. They insisted on maintaining the highest standards, if only to avoid them falling into the same trap as they had.

This is the milieu that James found himself as he progressed through childhood. He and his brother were expected to conform rigidly to a set of rules based literally on the teaching of the Bible and the guidance of the pastor at the local Baptist church. There was no question of allowing some freedom of choice. Rather, they lived by the dictum; *"do as I say or be damned."* Ironically this led to an improvement in the church community's attitude toward the parents. They were now being congratulated as an example of a complete turnaround from a previous life of sin to responsible parenthood.

To the father, nothing was more sinful than a homosexual relationship and he constantly repeated this to all who will listen, most especially to his children. He stated repeatedly that he would rather shoot any one of them than ever accept this abomination. He never hesitated to use any of the many major derogatory remarks against anyone suspected of this behavior nor was he ever shy in publicly condemning them. Like the majority of his generation, he has no idea of the prevailing thinking or trends and is adamantly opposed to change.

It was in this negative environment that that young James apparently found himself as he grew from childhood into adolescence and began to recognize his attraction to same sex individuals. Although there is no way of being certain, it appears that while his male peers would speak excitingly about their exploits with girls he felt nothing in common. Rather, for some unexplained reason, he might have found himself attracted by the sight of the male physique, especially older ones. In such a situation, it is not unreasonable to expect that it was only a matter of time before he met and developed a relationship with a young man, several years older. He knew that society still frowns upon this behavior, and particularly in his situation with regard to his father's outspoken antagonism, he would have known that he was standing at the edge of a volcano that can erupt at any time. But yet I can reasonably presume that he found it difficult, if not impossible, to change his deep inner feelings. He knew he must be discrete as the relationship developed and it remained so for a long time.

But in these modern times, with the advent of the internet with its ease and rapidity of communications and the real possibility of instantaneous exposure that can be broadcast literally as it occurs, the chance of maintaining discretion or secrecy does not exist. When one adds to this the multitude of social media outlets inhabited and utilized almost continuously by everyone, compounded by the universality of texting and the ease of multiple *Facetime* connections, it becomes readily understandable that secrets do not and cannot survive anymore. This is the world that today's younger generation must inhabit and must navigate through. A world that is so full of hidden minefields and so accessible to the scorching lights of exposure that it is virtually impossible to maintain privacy.

Against this background, it did not require a great leap forward to predict that sooner or later James's secret will be found out. From what information available, I can only suspect, without being absolutely certain, that most people were discrete and were quite prepared to keep their comments to themselves. Others went further, adopting a protective role by suppressing comments. Yet others adopted a supporting position choosing to neutralize any negative comments they encountered. Some went further by taking steps to warn James of the developing rumors and yet others even tried to offer friendly corrective suggestions. But, as expected in such situations, a few were not only delighted to receive this news but even more excited to embellish and spread it as far and as wide as they possibly could. One of these might have been Ritchie, the school bully, who hated James because of his popularity among his peers. Ritchie, the son of a prominent local attorney, resented any of his more successful fellow students. He genuinely felt that he deserved much more attention. He was very unpopular among his peers, both male and female, and sought revenge whenever and wherever the opportunity arose. As soon as the news fell at his feet it is suggested, though never confirmed, Ritchie did not hesitate to use it to the best of his scheming ability. He might have threatened James with publicly exposing his secret. He had not decided whether he will use *Facebook* or *Twitter*, suggesting he might use both for greater impact. Typically, he would proceed to make a handful of demands that were nothing short of blackmail, which he knew James could not satisfy. This might have been when James knew that he was in trouble!

All of a sudden, James could have felt that his world was crashing around him. He would be frightened, not so much for choosing an alternative lifestyle, but much more from the resulting turmoil that it will cause. Few people are broad-minded enough to truly understand and he was sure that his father's reaction would be at best, totally unacceptable and unmanageable. He would not appreciate, nor would he give his son an opportunity to explain himself. Instead he would probably rant and rave, quoting the words of Pastor Simeon about the sin and abomination his son had brought into his home and the punishment that God would extract from him. James understandably could have felt that he could not take the verbal and physical abuse that would inevitably occur.

To compound an already untenable situation, I suspect that his friend was not only unhelpful, but rather showed no interest in supporting him. He instead told him that he was on his own and moved on. There would be no one else to turn to! He would have thought that he could not confide in any of his teachers, and even if he tried, he doubted if any of them were willing or able to help. He knew the principal was of no help, he was more obsessed in producing good scores than in the welfare of his students. -Like it or not, he must have felt that he was on his own!

This is the frame of mind that might have overwhelmed him as he rode his bicycle home at the end of the school day on Friday. He might have feared that Ritchie will carry out his threat to "out" him on *Facebook* and publish a video he claimed he possessed, no later than Saturday and he knew he was defenseless to stop him. He would surely have known that if that occurs his life would become an endless hell and he just was not ready to live through this. He prayed for guidance but obviously found none. The only thought that could have dominated his mind was that his life was finished and there was nothing he can do to help himself. Even his favorite dinner, spaghetti and meatballs, could not help to cheer him much. Presumably the next few hours crept by as he remained immersed in this dark cloud of despair with the recurring thought of "I'm finished, I'm finished" playing like a broken record over and over, until he fell asleep.

What happened afterwards still remains a matter of conjecture, but my guess is that this was a repeat of an incident that took place some months earlier to one of my own patients who unsuccessfully attempted to commit suicide by swallowing a bottle full of her mother's pills and survived. When asked what made her take such a drastic step, she replied:

"I did it on a sudden impulse, when I could not bear the thought that everybody will soon know about me. It seemed that this was the right thing to do especially since none of my family or friends really understood."

I suspect that this was in fact the same mechanism that could have operated at 3 am on that Saturday morning when James awoke after a restless sleep. As is most often the case in Adolescent Suicide attempts, the action is almost invariably impulsive and very rarely pre-planned. The real tragedy is that in the cases of those lucky ones who survive, they invariably express genuine gratitude for not succeeding. I can only lament that if James had known this, or was lucky enough to have encountered the right individual who would have provided the appropriate guidance to him and his father, the outcome would have been so much different. But alas this was not the case and possibly as a result, a beautiful soul with so much to live for, was lost forever.

Less than two months earlier, a young man, distantly related to James, who was in his early twenty's, parked his car in a local shopping plaza packed with people shopping for the upcoming Christmas season. He connected the car's exhaust with a long plastic tube into the car and with the engine running went to sleep, never to awake. And less than 2 weeks after this event, Jack, James's school friend only a year older, was found hanging from a magnificent Oak tree in the forest outside of town by his friends.

-But these are both stories that must be told at a later date. Suffice it for me to note that except for the special details of the action taken, the circumstances surrounding each of these were essentially unchanged, as indeed has been our reaction. Perhaps it is high time that we begin to seriously heed the plea made by Pastor Sebastian at the James's funeral as he lamented yet another tragic loss within the congregation:

"Our tragedy is that we have not yet learned that we can and should do a lot more to help our young, vulnerable people over these periods of hopelessness. We can help to reduce the feeling that forces them to

believe that there is no way out, and we can avoid the senseless loss of so many of our children. The only problem we have is this:
......When are we going to make the effort to learn?"

I Saw no Lights at the end of the Tunnel
And No Angels Came to Visit

remember the evening of Sunday 27ᵗʰ of April very well. I had been given the OK by Dr. B. to go home next morning and we were all over-joyed that the long and difficult journey was finally coming to an end. Gloria, my dear devoted wife of 49 years was ecstatic beyond words. For not only was her husband, and soul-mate, coming home, but she was going to be spared of any more of the long, tiring trips from home to hospital which started at 6:00 am each morning and ended at 11:00 – 12:00 pm each night. She had already begun to plan with our son and three daughters a homecoming to remember.

In early March I was diagnosed with severe Coronary Heart Disease, and admitted to hospital under the care of Dr. D. for urgent Coronary Bypass sur-gery. The surgery, which I was assured was going to be "a piece of cake", turned out to be one of the most challenging Dr. D. had encountered in his 30 years as a Cardiac Surgeon. Instead of completing his task in the usual 2-3 hours, he spent over 6 hours before he felt comfortable. He had to replace 6 vessels instead of the 2-3 he had anticipated. During the surgery I had to be resuscitated twice and required 4 units of blood.

My post-surgical course was extremely rocky, to say the least. I suffered from literally every complication you could think of and as result, a usual stay of one week stretched out to 24 days up to April 27ᵗʰ. But thank God, this was all over and I was beginning to enjoy the thought of going home again. It was a good feeling indeed!

I don't recall what happened that night, and for that matter, what happened during the next 24 hours of my life. I can only recount what others have told me.

Gloria, who lived through every minute of the time, is convinced that God had a direct hand in this and that he was not ready for me yet.

-I am not willing to challenge this!

It would appear that what happened to me that night can only be described a "perfect storm" of events which together conspired to shut down all my systems. Everything started at about 5:00 am on Monday 28th when Nurse U, a fellow islander with whom I had struck up a relationship, decided to come up to the 6th floor from the 3rd floor where she worked, to visit me. She found me deeply comatose and unresponsive and immediately called a "Code Blue" as she proceeded to initiate CPR. Within minutes the code team had assembled, led by two of the most experienced and competent personnel in the hospital. There was Dr. M, a short, diminutive Latin-born Intensivist with the worst possible bedside manner I have ever encountered, but with an aggressive and totally uncompromising attitude to succeed at all cost and to stay with it until success is assured. And there was Nurse I, a male nurse and team leader, who went beyond his call of duty and stayed with me long after his shift was finished seeing that orders were carried out expeditiously. He left only when he felt I had passed the danger. Here again, Gloria is convinced that the hand of God was at work, for it was the general consensus that many of the other teams would have given up earlier.

-Again, who am I to challenge this!

My recall of the activities that had begun at 5:00am, March 28th and continued on into the next day is vague and disjointed. My mind was playing tricks on me and I could not explain or understand anything going on around me. In some ways it felt like a weird dream involving people and places that I knew and recognized. And at other times I felt a strange out-of-body experience as if I was a bystander objectively looking on at the activities unfolding, accepting what was going on without knowing why. I somehow recognized that this was a hospital room, but it did not look or feel like any hospital room I knew. There were people all around, but I never made out the faces of anyone in the room. But in the middle of all this, I clearly recalled (subsequently confirmed) the voice of my nephew, Dr. J, who had hurried to hospital upon receiving a phone call from Gloria and was actively participating in my resuscitation. I distinctly heard him whispering into my left ear, *"Uncle, stay with me, stay with me. You will be OK".* That was the only voice I heard throughout my ordeal, although I am told the room was overflowing with personnel, medical and non-medical, including, I am told, the Chaplain who was summoned by Gloria.

After I had fully recovered, everyone was amazed that I had retained all my faculties. My cognitive functions and my memory seemed to be intact, as was my sense of humor. It seems that I had merely recovered from a long sleep. However, I disappointed a lot of people because I could not confirm for them that I had entered a tunnel, or had seen a light or had seen the face of Jesus or was visited by an Angel. I have no recollection of any such occurrences.

But then I also respect the wisdom and deep faith of my wife, Gloria, who counters the enquirers by asking:

"Do we have to see a light, or walk in a tunnel or touch an Angel to know that the hand of God was present throughout?"

-A question I cannot possibly challenge!

In the end all I can say in good conscience, is that I saw no lights at the end of a tunnel, and no Angel came to visit me but I certainly went on a journey to remember,

... And I am grateful that I came back!

My Spiritual love

*M*any years ago, while I was still a young man who felt that he could, and will conquer the world, I attended the 60th wedding anniversary of my late uncle. He was a man whom I held, and still do, in the highest possible regard for the depth of wisdom as well as the extent of knowledge, experience and qualities of life he displayed. Indeed, he was my "Guru", whose advice I sought, whose opinions I cherished, and whose life I admired and still try to emulate. I have always attributed much of the success in my career and my life to his wisdom, his advice and his example. So much so, that I have attempted to pass these principles on to my own children in every way I can.

He began his speech by describing marriage as:

> *"A journey which begins with physical attraction then crosses several stages of Love and Commitment, to arrive at the ultimate level of Spiritual Love".*

Over the succeeding years I have often reflected on that statement and wondered what he really meant by "Spiritual Love."

I believe I find the answer each time I see a particular television advertisement depicting an elderly couple walking slowly, hand in hand, along a garden pathway, serenely oblivious of the world around them, totally content with their own life, wanting and needing nothing more. Then a young couple who have clearly only recently found each other, briskly passes them and look back in total admiration and respect. I am convinced that that they too, have arrived at that exalted place.

And for me, after more than 50 years of marriage, sharing my life with my wife, being blessed with a family of 4 children and a life overflowing with good memories, I believe I too, am beginning to truly understand what he meant by *"Spiritual Love"*;

"It is the unspoken word that speaks volumes.
It is the smile, however fleeting, that says 'thank you',
And the frown, however brief, that stops you.
It is the feeling of joy and security whenever she appears, however
many times she does.
And the momentary regret, when she leaves the room.
It is knowing what she thinks and wants, before her saying so,
And equally, It is being certain that she will respond to my requests,
even before I had requested.
It is the warm feeling that flows over me whenever she is with me,
And the deep sadness I feel whenever she hurts or she is not well.

Above all, it is my constant desire to thank God, over and over, for this gift of my soul-mate, and the profound hope that she will continue to grace my life for many more years."

< >

Being deeply loved by someone gives you strength;
Loving someone deeply gives you courage.
.... Lao Tzu

Love is the master key that opens the gates of Happiness.
........Oliver Wendell Holmes

Love would never be a promise of a rose garden,
unless it is showered with light of faith, water of sincerity and air of passion.
......Author Unknown

Love is, above all, the gift of oneself.
.......Jean Anouilh

Love is a gift of one's innermost soul to another;
......So both can be whole
...... Tea Rose

Married couples who love each other tell each other a thousand things;
-Without talking.
.....Chinese Proverb

For True love is inexhaustible;
The more you give, the more you have.
And if you go to draw at the true fountainhead,
the more water you draw, the more abundant is its flow.
...... Antoine de Saint-Exupery

This is the miracle that happens every time to those who really love;
The more they give, the more they possess
To love and to be loved is the greatest happiness of existence.
.... Sydney Smith

Love still remains when you lose everything else; ... Even life.
.....Anastasia Sabga

SECTION 2

Individual Expressions

Our basic emotions, our individual expressions are the main drivers of our lives.

How we live and how we choose to express ourselves determines the quality of life we enjoy.

We are not creatures of logic but creatures of emotion and as such our lives are determined by influences that are basically outside of our consciousness.

To the outside world we are what we project. We are indeed a mirror of our expressions and we are perceived as what we appear to be, not what we think we are.

Life with Jealousy and Envy

"Jealousy is the jaundice of the soul".

*C*ontrary to popular belief, Jealousy combined with Envy is not merely a negative instinctive emotion or attitude that can affect everyone. Rather, it should be seen as an all consuming way of life that ultimately devours and destroys a person's self-esteem as well as his relationship with others. No human emotion can do as much damage to oneself and one's environment as Jealousy unchecked. We see evidence of this every day all around us.

Throughout the ages, civilizations and religions have universally condemned jealousy as an evil and undesirable emotion. Some of the most disastrous wars have been fought because of jealousy and envy. History is replete with examples of extreme actions taken by leaders to justify their basic jealousy and envy. More people have suffered directly or indirectly at the hands of jealousy than all the natural disasters in the world put together.

The Holy Bible in *Song of Solomon 8:6-7* records:

"Jealousy is cruel as the grave:
The coals thereof are coals of fire,
which hath a most vehement flame".

The Holy Quran, in *Riyadh-us-Salaheen Hadith 1569*, quotes the Prophet Muhammed:

> *"Avoid jealousy, for it destroys*
> *good deeds as fire destroys wood."*

Buddha in his wisdom, advises:

> *"Do not overrate what you have received, nor envy others.*
> *He who envies others does not obtain peace of mind".*

Yet despite all of the experiences and the admonitions of the religions, jealousy remain the strongest and most potent of all the emotions, and continues to exert its negative force on humanity, causing untold pain and suffering to all and sundry.

Nowadays we tend to conflate the separate terms of Jealousy and Envy and use them interchangeably, but traditionally they are quite distinct, each eliciting different emotional responses;

> Jealousy is the emotion experienced when an individual felt that a relationship or possession was threatened, or an anticipated loss of something they desired or when attention is directed away from them.
>
> Envy, describes the externalized threat. It is the feelings experienced by one who longed for the possessions or attributes of another, or resented an advantage enjoyed by another person.

Nevertheless irrespective of which one of these is the primary focus, it inevitably incorporates the other to produce a global response affecting the total person. And once started it will, like a rapidly spreading cancer, continue to grow to involve a person's whole psyche and his relationship with others, leading to increasing suspicion, avoidance and isolation. We can all relate to these states not only because of our experiences with others, but because to a greater or lesser extent we are all guilty of being jealous and envious on many and diverse occasions. Most of the time, these emotions are learned responses and have their origin in early experiences, especially related to parental attitudes and influences. Many experts suggest that there may be an inherited component, pointing to the commonly regarded fact that *"it runs in families"*.

Whatever the etiology however, there is no doubt that the long term consequences of uncontrolled or uncorrected jealousy and envy are personality destruction, distrust and isolation. It is interesting to note that these emotions do exist in the animal kingdom as well and at times may lead to major conflicts within the animal groups.

Overcoming jealousy and envy can be exceedingly difficult and sometimes almost impossible. It requires a self awareness by the individual that the attitudes and actions are wrong and a need to come to terms with this. Unfortunately because these feelings are associated with underlying fear and anger, it becomes very difficult to achieve effective change. In the end, many of the victims unfortunately tend to avoid contact or be avoided. Which ever way this turns, they end up becoming increasingly isolated.

In this context, I was attracted to the following verse which is included in a poem in a current blog under the authorship of *Rajwinraj*. It very effectively summarizes the outcome of Jealousy uncorrected:

> *"Jealousy is anger, jealousy is hate*
> *Jealousy may lurk behind any hidden gate,*
> *Jealousy is deadly, under the night sky*
> *Jealousy is a poison that many die by".*

> *Anger is cruel and fury overwhelming,*
> *But who can stand before Jealousy.*
> *......Proverbs 27:4*

> *There is no greater glory than love,*
> *nor any greater punishment than jealousy.*
> *...Lope de Vega*

It is not love that is blind, but jealousy.
........*Lawrence Durrell,*

The Jealous bring down the curse they fear upon their own heads.
........*Dorothy Dix*

The jealous are troublesome to others, but a torment to themselves.
......*William Penn*

Jealousy is the tie that binds, and binds, and binds.
........*Helen Rowland*

Envy slays itself by its own arrows.
........*Author Unknown*

*Our envy always lasts longer than
the happiness of those we envy.*
.......*François Duc de La Rochefoucauld*

*As iron is eaten by rust,
so are the envious consumed by envy.*
.......*Antisthenes*

Life with Humility

"*Humility oftentimes conjures up images of weakness, submissiveness, and fear. -But this is a false idea of humility. Real humility is a sign of strength, authentic confidence, and courage. It is the mark of a true man.*"

This comment by an author whose identity is unknown perfectly encapsulates the true meaning of humility. It is one we all will do well to take to heart. Humility exists at two completely contrasting levels;

-On one level, it is a state of being humble or having a low esteem of oneself or tending to project an image of inferiority. It is a feeling that one is less important than others.

-And on the other hand, Humility is a virtue, a position of strength and confidence without a need to advertise, to be pretentious or to be disrespectful of another.

Both Confucius, the ancient Chinese philosopher, and St. Augustine, whose life was a study in humility, described it as "*the foundation of all other virtues*". In fact, throughout the ages and in every civilization, the one most constant characteristic of many of the respected and successful leaders, thinkers, scientists and teachers is that of humility. All the major religions emphasize repeatedly the importance of humility in the lives of the followers;

In Christianity, consider the life of Jesus, the Son of God. He chose to be born into the family of a poor carpenter, in a stable among animals, and live for most of his life on earth in poverty. And when he began to preach the Doctrine of Heaven he was ridiculed, accused of blasphemy and ignored by the establishment. In the end he was treated like a criminal, tortured and crucified between two thieves. He endured all of this with humility and forgiveness in his heart. His message was clear and indelibly imprinted to all who believe, that entry into the kingdom can be achieved only by humility and forgiveness. The constant theme in the Bible and all Christian literature attests to the overriding emphasis of humility among the disciples, prophets, saints, leaders and teachers in their lives and thought, so much so that the Christianity is often called *the Doctrine of Humility.*

In Judaism, humility is considered an indispensable ingredient in the religious and social perspective. The Torah contains many references to humility being deeply associated with the complex system of Jewish ethics. Rabbi Jonathan Sacks, Chief Rabbi for Great Britain and the Commonwealth, in his excellent essay entitled *On Humility,* expressed his profound sentiments in the following manner:

> *"Humility, true Humility, is one of the most expansive and life-enhancing of all virtues. It does not mean undervaluing yourself. It means valuing other people. It signals a certain openness to life's grandeur and the willingness to be surprised and uplifted by goodness wherever one finds it".*

In Islam, Muslims are encouraged to practice the daily Islamic virtues of modesty, submission and respect, and to reject pride and arrogance. The act of prostration at pray five times a day acknowledges a person's humility and lowliness before the world. The Holy Quran advises the practitioner to *"Call Allah in humility"* to prevent suffering and adversity.

In Buddhism, Humility leads to being liberated from the sufferings of life and all illusions of stress and self-deception by achieving the freedom of *Nirvana.* Enlightenment can come only after humility, which ultimately leads to wisdom.

I have no doubt that each one of us can readily think of many examples of people with true humility with whom we have come in contact or about whom we have read or heard about. For my own self, of the many people who have crossed my path or about whom I have acquired knowledge, I will identify two persons whose life has been spent in total humility despite having to deal with enormous obstacles.

The first is His *Holiness the Dalai Lama XIV*, who has been forced to live in exile since 1959 when the Chinese invaded Tibet. Despite profound deprivations suffered by him and his followers, he continues to preach peace, love and forgiveness to all. Although he has met leaders of most of the nations of the world, this has in no way affected his self-image and he continues to shine with the aura of humility. The following quotation speaks volumes on his views on life:

> *"Every day, think as you wake up, today I am fortunate to be alive, I have a precious human life. I am not going to waste it. I am going to use all my energies to develop myself, to expand my heart out to others; I will achieve enlightenment for the benefit of all beings. I am going to have kind thoughts towards others, I am not going to get angry or think badly about others. I am going to benefit others as much as I can."*

The second is *Blessed Teresa of Kolkata*, the Romanian-born Roman Catholic nun who spent all her life caring for the sick, the poor and the needy of India and of the world. She was recognized and honored by leaders of many countries for her contributions to improving the suffering of the people, but never ever lost sight of the paramount value of humility. She expressed her concept of humility in the following terms:

> *"Humility is the mother of all virtues; purity, charity and obedience. It is in being humble that our love becomes real, devoted and ardent. If you are humble nothing will touch you, neither praise nor disgrace, because you know what you are. If you are blamed you will not be discouraged. If they call you a saint you will not put yourself on a pedestal."*

In 1985, Michael Jackson and Lionel Ritchie co-wrote a song entitled *"We are the World"* that was performed on stage by a large group of prominent entertainers as part of international aid program for Africa. It began with the following words:

"There comes a time when we must heed a certain call;
When the world must come together as one."

Sometimes I wonder how beautiful this world of ours will become if somehow the leaders and the people of the world could come together in common humility and truly heed the advice and example of these gifted people.

---But alas, I realize, that this is only a dream that will never see the light of day.

When pride comes, then comes disgrace;
But with Humility comes wisdom.
.......Proverbs 11:2

Do nothing out of selfish ambition or vain conceit,
but in Humility consider others better than yourselves.
......Philippians 2:3

Life is a long lesson in humility
......James M. Barrie

Humility makes great men twice honorable
.........Benjamin Franklin.

We come nearest to the great,
when we are great in humility
.......Rubindranath Tagore

Humility leads to strength, not weakness.
It is the highest from of self-respect.
.......John McCloy

In truth there's nothing so becomes a man
as modest stillness and humility.
.....William Shakespeare

Humility is the only true wisdom by which we prepare our minds for
all the possible changes of life.
......George Arliss

Life is a long lesson in Humility.
......James M. Barrie

It is no great thing to be Humble when you are brought low;
But to be Humble when you are praised is a great and rare
attainment.
........St. Bernard of Clairvaux

Humility, like the darkness, reveals heavenly lights.
......Henry David Thoreau

Humility is not thinking less of you,
It's thinking of you less.
.....Timothy Keller

Life after Failure and Defeat

"The successes of today are built, not on the results of early successes,
but upon the back of earlier failures."

This statement was made by Sumner Redstone, a leading American Businessman, Media Magnate and Philanthropist, several years ago in his autobiography. It has impressed me so much that I have included it in my list of core quotations.

The history of man throughout the ages is overflowing with examples of this. To my knowledge many, if not all, of the most successful people have arrived at the top by traveling on a road strewn with multiple rocks of failure.

-As a young man, Abraham Lincoln went to war as a captain and returned a private. He failed in several business ventures and as a Lawyer was only able to earn money by becoming an itinerant attorney. As a politician, he was no less successful. He was defeated in his attempt to be elected to congress, and twice to the senate as well. In his first attempt for the vice-presidency, he lost miserably. Yet as the 16th President he successfully presided over the most difficult period of American History.

-Winston Churchill failed as a student, was defeated in every election for public office (although he was appointed to several cabinet posts), until his election as Prime Minister in 1940. His leadership is credited with saving England in WWII. In addition he became an accomplished artist, historian and author, recognized worldwide.

-Henry Ford, founder of the Ford Motor Company and father of the modern assembly lines used in mass production, failed and went broke five times before he succeeded. He publicly recorded this experience and his reason to continue, thus:

Failure is only the opportunity to begin again,
This time, more intelligently.

-Sigmund Freud, the father of Psychotherapy, was booed from the podium when he first presented his ideas to the scientific community. But he eventually gained much respect and acceptance because of his commitment and persistence.

-Walt Disney, the greatest entertainment mogul that the world has ever seen, failed miserably on several business ventures, including declaring bankrupt in 1922, before finally launching his immensely successful Disney Entertainment World.

The great majority of people are so concerned with failure that they approach challenges with undue trepidation and caution. The thought of failure weighs so heavily on them that many potentially successful ventures never see the light of day. To them the *"shame of failure"* is just not acceptable. I recall my own father spending long hours in deep thought and concern over a business opportunity because of the risk of failing. Had it not been for the persistence of his brother-in-law he might well have walked away from what became a very successful venture.

Having said that, we must not lose sight of the fact that these people described as *"extra cautious and conservative,"* form the backbone of our society, and are the ones responsible for its successful and predictable conduct. In fact, the survival of society is more directly dependant on them than on the "reckless" pursuits of the risk takers. Without them, chaos and confusion will prevail and the orderly conduct of the day to day activities of society will not exist nor for that matter, will the risk taker succeed.

Although society universally frowns on risk takers who fail, the truth is that the most successful and the most progressive leaders and entrepreneurs are found among the risk takers and failure-prone. That indeed, is the secret weapon of all successful people. They see the risk of failure is, like so many other intangibles, just part of doing business. Failure is merely a pause from which they will learn lessons to help them to try again.

All of us can no doubt think of instances of people who have come back from embarrassing defeat to achieve resounding success later in life. I recall my earliest and most impressive example occurred when I was less than 10 years old. I clearly recall the circumstance when one of my father's very close friends announced to him one Sunday morning, that his business had failed and he was forced to declare bankruptcy at the age of 55. Undaunted he started a new business and by dint of commitment and hard work grew it into a multi-million dollar success within a few years. Several years later I asked him the reason for his success, his reply was simply: *"I learnt from losing everything."*

In 1980, as a result of a series of events, some predictable, others beyond my control, and despite attaining substantial success, both socially and professionally, I made the decision to relocate. The move, at best, was daunting, the pressure upon my wife and young family was formidable and the uncertainty of the future course was substantial. However, despite several periods of wavering doubt in my mind, I knew that defeat was never an option. Ultimately success was achieved, beyond my expectations. I learnt more about myself during this period than at any other time of my life. I learnt the true wisdom of a motto that had been my late father's, and continues to be a favorite of my own. It is one that I willingly pass on to my children:

"It does not matter how many times you fall.
What matters is that you get up each time you do.
-You will fail only when you do not get up"

Paul Tillich, the Christian Theologian and Philosopher was truly inspired when he recorded the following statement:

"He who risks and fails can be forgiven.
He who never risks and never fails
is a failure in his whole being."

Failure is success if we learn from it.
.....Malcolm S. Forbes

It is fine to celebrate success, but
It is more important to heed the lessons of failure
....Bill Gates

The men who try to do something and fail are infinitely better
than those who try to do nothing and succeed.
.....Lloyd Jones

Rather fail with honor than succeed by Fraud.
...Sophocles

No man is a failure who has friends.
....Clarence, (Movie: "It's a Wonderful Life")

Life with Honor

"Life, every man holds dear.
But the dear man holds Honor far more precious than life."

The above statement written by William Shakespeare in one of his lesser known tragedies, *Troilus and Cressida*, defines the true meaning of Honor among men.

Honor can be defined in many ways. Basically it is the respect and esteem earned by an individual through deed and reputation. It does not however mean an automatic recognition of one's right to great respect, and does not come by simply doing remarkable things in impossible situations. Rather it comes by acquisition of respect among others, slowly. As good deeds accumulate respect turns in something more, and before you know it, the person has earned Honor.

Honor can also be subjective and relates to a person's Integrity. In plain language, an honorable person avoids using deception whenever possible, treats others with the respect they deserve and sticks to his beliefs no matter how others think or act. This is a priceless gift that anyone in the world can achieve. It cannot be bought, or sold or traded, and can only be earned by acknowledgement of his peers. It is a code of behavior, characterized by a pattern of ethical and moral conduct, loyalty and integrity. It means establishing a reputation and a moral identity that are consistent and predictable, and keeping these at all cost.

Honor cannot be passed on from generation to generation, nor can it be learnt from reading books. It however can be taught by example and model, and by providing the right milieu. A child growing up in a home where respect, loyalty and commitment are the norm will have a better chance of developing these principles than one who does not. Similarly, a society which recognizes the importance of Honor is more likely to produce similar behavior among its members than one which does not.

In my own life, for as long as I can recall, the concept of Honor has been an integral part of my life. Growing up in a home where I witnessed my father who lived by his word and took every opportunity to impart this to his children, it seemed quite easy to follow. He often related to us his reason why he Gave up his family name and adopted his middle name. This was because of the behavior of his cousins and namesakes. Their actions were unacceptable to him and he could not condone nor risk being associated with them. To me this action was totally commendable and appropriate, though many others disagreed.

Throughout my life, I have encountered many men of honor and have consistently admired and respected the way they conducted their lives. By contrast, I have been associated with many others who spent their lives in deceitful, selfish gain and unprincipled behavior and who have earned and continue to earn my unreserved contempt. I can think of one family, whose offspring have consistently lived by deceit, manipulation and scheming and who have the uncanny ability to pass this on to subsequent generations. Although highly successful in the eyes of society, their lives are strewn with an unending series of disastrous relationships and hardships. Their stories can be used to illustrate the real dangers of sacrificing Honor on the altar greed and deceit.

In the end however, I believe that to live with honor is a very personal choice that cannot be passed on to others who are unwilling to accept the choice. No amount of explanation or reasoning will effect a change. With apologies to the original author, I believe that I could express this more clearly by adapting a very famous quotation by Nancy Gibbs, a former editor of TIME magazine:

> *"For those who live with Honor, no explanation is necessary.*
> *For those who don't, no explanation is possible."*

Be honorable yourself if you wish to associate with honorable people.
.....Welsh Proverb

The difference between a Moral man and a Man of Honor
is that the latter regrets a discreditable act;
even when it has worked and he has not been caught.
.......H.L. Menken

Be not ashamed of thy virtues;
Honor is a good brooch to wear in a man's hat at all times.
...Ben Johnson

A life spent making mistakes is not only more Honorable,
but more useful than a life spent doing nothing.
.........George Bernard Shaw

Honor does not have to be defended.
......Robert J. Sawyer

If you stand straight, do not fear a crooked shadow.
.....Chinese Proverb

A man has Honor if he holds himself to an ideal of conduct;
-Though it may be inconvenient, unprofitable, or dangerous to do so.
.......Walter Lippman

Integrity is not a conditional word. It doesn't blow in the wind or
change with the weather. It is your inner image of yourself.
And if you look in there and see a man who won't cheat;
Then you know he never will.
......Author Unknown

Life with Faith

"Faith is not necessary when you know how things are going to work out, that's Knowledge. It's in the time of unknowing, that having faith is what sees you through to the other side. Faith is what gives you strength. It is that light in your heart that keeps on shining even when it's all darkness outside. Now is the time to keep that faith alive!"

*M*any years ago I came across this description of Faith by an unnamed author in a blog managed by *Synthia F. Jones*, a mother of three, a business woman, full-time college student, and a visionary. Since then, it has remained the standard by which I define Faith's true meaning. It refers especially, to faith possessed by an individual that leads to expression of confidence in a person, or a plan or an idea. The result is an unshakable trust that the outcome will always be favorable.

In the Religious setting, Faith describes belief in certain ideas, or conditions or in a super-natural power that ultimately controls human thought and destiny. It is the basis of the fundamental differences between the various religions and is most often the cause and reason for the continued separate identities. The major common denominators within all the religions such as love, respect, understanding, tolerance and good works are generally similar and interchangeable. However, these are deliberately understated in favor of contrasting dogmas of faith, in order to maintain and propagate their differences and ensure continued disagreements. One should therefore not be surprised at the ongoing interreligious strife and disharmony.

True faith should play an integral role in all aspects of our lives. Not just on our religious beliefs, but in everything we do and in everyone we encounter. When faith is operating there is a deep-seated trust that the right way will always appear. There will be a shield of security that protects you from fears of human failing, loss or disappointment. It provides a feeling of calm and confidence that comes from trusting entirely to the truth, and embracing and committing to the truth in all things. The truth itself will become your faith.

St. Augustine of Hippo, the great philosopher and theologian, who lived in the 4th century AD, one of the most important figures in the development of Western Christianity, was one of the earliest to consider and investigate the importance of Faith in life. Born of a Pagan father and a Christian mother he spent his early years as a staunch pagan following the teachings of Manes and Plato until his "conversion" to Catholicism in 386 AD. From then on he became a prolific writer and teacher on all aspects of religion. His most famous publication was the *Enchridion,* a handbook on Christian theology in which he wrote extensively on Faith and its importance to Christian Life. He concluded the publicastion by recording a simple but very powerful observation:

"Faith is to believe what you do not see.
-The reward of this faith is to see what you believe".

Throughout the ages, Faith has been the constant companion of all the great leaders, teachers, thinkers, authors, religious, and successful people who have excelled in their chosen fields. Ask anyone of them the reason for their success and the universal response will invariably be the faith in themselves. A cursory look at their writings on the subject will confirm, beyond any question, the dominating role played by faith in every successful individuals. In fact, I am convinced that in the great majority of instances, Faith by the individual is the singular driving force to success.

But faith is not only for the few, it is within the reach of anyone of us. Whether we are able to call upon it however depends on many diverse factors such as experience, example, personality, environment and exposure. We are all able to readily recognize many examples in our own lives or in the lives of others around us where the presence of faith was the over-riding phenomenon. In my own practice over many years, I have never failed to marvel at the rapidity of recovery and the significant improvement of many of my patients which can be directly related to the depth of their faith. In fact, several large scale studies have confirmed the validity of this observation in respect to such varying conditions as post surgical recovery, post-stroke, drug and alcohol abuse and depression. It is unfortunate that we, as physicians, are not trained and are generally insensitive to this aspect of recovery. It can be a potent ally in the management of our patients.

Even in our daily living, Faith can play a significant role in our life. It can influence our thinking, provide stability and aid us in making meaningful decisions that are not colored by inner fears and inadequacies. It induces a sense of security and confidence that clearly goes a long way in aiding us to avoid the pitfalls of uncertainty. In many ways it can be viewed as the foundation of success. In this respect, I can do no better than to offer an adaptation of a much repeated quotation by the great African-American educator and civil-rights leader, founder of the Bethune-Cookman University and advisor to President Franklin D. Roosevelt, *Mary Jane McLeod Bethune:*

"Without faith, nothing is possible. With faith, nothing is impossible."

Now Faith is the assurance of things hoped for,
the conviction of things not seen.
........Hebrews11:1

Be faithful in small things because,
It is in them that your strength lies.
........Mother Teresa

Faith is a passionate intuition.
.......William Wordsworth

Faith is taking the first step;
even when you don't see the whole staircase.
....Martin Luther King

Faith is not belief. Belief is passive. Faith is active.
........Edith Hamilton

I do not pray for success; I ask for faithfulness.
.....Mother Teresa

Faith is believing.
-Even when it is beyond the power of reason to believe.
......Voltaire

It's lack of Faith that makes you afraid to meet challenges.
.....Muhammed Ali

Life with Loneliness

*K*halil Gibran in his book *A Second Treasury*, a brilliantly written observation on life, very accurately and beautifully described the true role of loneliness in the context of living, in the following manner:

> *"Life is an island in an ocean of loneliness. It is an island whose rocks are hopes, whose trees are dreams, whose flowers are solitude, and whose brooks are thirst. Your life, my fellow men, is an island separated from other islands and regions. No matter how many are the ships that leave your shores for other climes, no matter how many are the fleets that touch your coast, you remain a solitary island, suffering the pangs of loneliness and yearning for happiness.*
>
> *You are unknown to your fellow man and far removed from their sympathy and understandings"*

Loneliness is a state of feeling cut off from, and a longing for, others. It results from the avoidance or absence of physical or emotional contact with people, whether these are loved ones, friends, or acquaintances. This is not to be confused with Solitude or choosing to be alone. Here the individual voluntarily chooses isolation for personal reasons and as a result involuntarily finds himself in a state of isolation. While being alone can be a very positive and rewarding experience, especially when used as a time of reflection, contemplation and self-evaluation, and can often lead to personal growth and enhancement, Loneliness is a totally different state of affairs. The profound feelings of isolation and rejection, the pain of losing your contacts and social networks and the inability to communicate with others can lead to intense feelings of inadequacy, anxiety and depression, and can seriously compromise physical and mental well-being.

Loneliness is a universal human response. None of us are immune from episodes of loneliness and I am sure anyone of us will have no difficulty in readily identifying instances of loneliness that have left indelible effects on our psyche. It has no single cause, nor does it respect age, sex, intellectual ability or socioeconomic status. It is complex and unique to the individual, and has a strong correlation to underlying personality and psychological characteristics. It exists all around us. We see it in our friends and family, among our neighbors and strangers and read about it in our books and newspapers. Unfortunately, although we will all have no difficulty in recognizing it and all its sequellae, it is rare that we are able to help others to successfully deal with its consequences.

Over the many years of my practice, I have seen loneliness present itself in all its many and varied faces. I have seen it in children, manifesting itself as apathy, withdrawal, as eating and bowel disorders, and even as aggressive and anti-social behavior. Some experts suggest that Autism is merely an extreme manifestation of Loneliness. Among adolescents, loneliness may well be the most common underlying factor in a large number of behavioral problems encountered. This is not surprising when one considers the enormous conflicts to which they are exposed and the ridiculous demands of our "modern" society. Quite often the consequences may be tragic as was the recent case of a young girl who was driven to committing suicide as a result of peer pressure and isolation. This situation is certainly not improved by the appearance of such popular community sites as *Facebook and Twitter* where loneliness becomes *"hidden in public view"*.

In adulthood and to a larger extent, among seniors, the problems of loneliness wreak havoc among the individuals and their families. With the added burdens associated with socio-economic distress, severe health problems and loss of life-long partners the incidence of loneliness and the resulting health and emotional deterioration become dominant and the resulting suffering, overwhelming. Is it any surprise that loneliness is often referred to as *"Scourge for all Seasons!"*

Whatever the cause, it is vitally important that immediate and urgent steps be taken to correct or reduce its impact. Every effort must be made to educate people on the early recognition, correction and prevention of this damaging state of mind. People in this state tend to feel increasingly empty and unwanted. Although they recognize the need for human contact, their state of mind actually makes it more difficult to do so and as a result they run an increased risk of developing serious health and mental problems.

Despite all we know about the subject, and how relatively easy it is to recognize its appearance and its effects I am sorry to note that as individuals or as a society we are doing very little to help. Much more was achieved in the past when people were closer, interdependence stronger and responsibility greater. *Sir Bertrand Russell*, one of Britain's greatest philosophers, historians, logicians, mathematicians and social critics who died in 1970 at the age of 97 years, reflected the thinking of that time When he wrote:

> *"Nature did not construct human beings to stand alone.*
> *Those who have never known the deep intimacy and intense companionship of happy mutual love have missed the best thing that life has to give. Love is the principal means of escape from loneliness, which afflicts most men and women throughout the greater part of their lives."*

-How disappointing that we could not, in good conscience, say that everything is being done to help these unfortunate people at this present time when we have much more ability to do so!

> *All the Lonely People, where do they all come from?*
> ....*John Lennon and Paul McCartney*
>
> *People are lonely because they build walls instead of bridges.*
> ....*Joseph F. Newton*
>
> *Loneliness is not a fault, but a condition of existence.*
> ....*Ivan Albright*

Loneliness and the feeling of being unwanted
is the most terrible poverty.
.......Mother Teresa

The surest cure for Vanity is Loneliness.
.......Thomas Wolfe

You cannot be alone,
if you like the person you are alone with.
.......Wayne Dyer

Nothing is more lamentable and sterile
than a man content to live alone.
....Harold Pinter

Life's Victories
A study in faith, strength and courage

*D*uring the month of October, my attention was drawn to a series of personal stories written by survivors of Breast Cancer in celebration of "Breast Cancer Month" in the local newspaper, under the heading *Life's Victories*. As a practicing Physician for more than 50 years I have treated and cared for many hundreds of cancer patients and have shared a variety of sad and painful and hopeful and happy moments with my patients and their family, all of which I cherish and thank God for granting me the opportunity to do so.

These stories impacted me more than I expected probably because in the last 18 to 24 months I found myself a concerned participant in such a battle. Ever since my wife was diagnosed with cancer of the breast I found that despite all the years of carefully cultivating the cloak of the "all knowing, unflappable, supportive physician always ready with the right advice or the right answer", I was as vulnerable and as reactive as anyone else and that I needed the same kind of support as I had offered to others. I found myself for the first time in a paradoxical "no-man's land". On the one hand as the physician, I was expected to know all and make all the right decisions, and as a husband and life partner, to be caring, supporting, encouraging and sharing with my wife as she navigated through the stormy seas of Surgeons and Oncologists and Mammograms and CT Scans and Pet Scans and Hospitals and Radiation and Chemotherapy. It was, and indeed is, a most humbling experience and one which, despite my many years of clinical experience, has taught me a great deal about my own inner humanity.

As I read these stories which were basically simple comments made from the heart by the survivors, I was struck by the strength and character of these people, who had resolutely endured the pain, suffering and uncertainty of their journey and came through stronger and more resilient. This clearly speaks volumes to the resilience of the human character and the ability to rise above the onslaught of adversity. I can do no better to honor these people than to provide a brief quote from a selected few of their many stories published under the banner of *"Life's Victories"*:

-*"To never give up hope, that breast cancer is not a death sentence, and to be sure to surround yourself around supportive, loving people".*
......Cindy

-*"My battle with cancer was an opportunity for me to learn so much about how my lifestyle choices can contribute to, or detract from, the health of my body, mind, and spirit".*
..... Genienne

-*"Don't assume someone else's experience will be yours. I can't say how many UNNECESSARY sleepless nights I had worried I was going to have side effects or pains that others talked about in forums that never came".*
..... Marsha

-*"In some ways breast cancer has been a positive experience for me. Having breast cancer has empowered me. I have strength & courage I never thought I had. I have gained so much knowledge regarding what is going on inside of my body & my appreciation for life is sky high. I have made the most wonderful friends. These are bonds that will never be broken".*
..... Abbe

-*"My advise to someone just diagnosed is to stay calm, it will be all right. This is just another chapter in your life. You will get through this with the help of your family and friends and loved ones.*
. .... Virginia

-"To anyone who is going through this experience, I recommend take one day at a time, and be positive. And remember: this too shall pass."
….. Marie

-"One of the best lessons I've learned is how beautiful people can be and that a positive attitude is one of the best drugs you can take".
…. Sandra

-"My advice is to find happiness in your life's purpose. Don't be afraid to be yourself. Make up your mind that you will survive. Be strong, proactive, collect information and make educated decisions".
…… Dawn

-"Through this journey I heard so many inspiring cancer survival stories that my outlook on life has changed. I want to enjoy life to the fullest and make myself as happy as possible because I am alive and well".
….. Kathleen

As for my wife, I continue to marvel at the calm and courageous demeanor that she has brought to bear as she continues on her journey to *"the cure"*. I have no doubt that a great deal of this is related to the caring competence and professionalism of her treating physicians and staff, and to the strong and unwavering support of her children, her family and her many loyal friends. But above all this, there is her unbending and overwhelming faith in her God, her destiny, and her belief that her God will never abandon her. Her favorite quotation to which she holds firmly and with conviction, is from *Book of Isaiah 43:2*:

"When you go through the sea, I am with you.
When you go through rivers, they will not sweep you away.
When you walk through fire, you will not be burned,
And the flames will not harm you".

Living with Forgiveness

"By not forgiving, you only build a high wall between
yourself and God.
This prevents his good graces from flowing back to you, and You be-
come filled with such negative feelings that consumes all of you,
as well as your relationship with everyone else."

These words were spoken by my cousin Starr Sabga during a discussion on the evils of *not forgiving* others. In her simple but direct manner, she focused directly on the true effect this action has on us and our life situation. Like a rotting fruit which, if not replaced destroys everything around it, so too will this affect everything we do, or think, or believe or expect. This results in us undergoing profound changes in our ability to relate with others or with ourselves. We become angry, suspicious and frustrated and quickly begin to mistrust people's intentions. Before long we even lose sight of the original conflict as we develop an ever widening circle of "enemies" in our lives. In short we become different persons with different outlooks and different expectations.

Forgiveness is a virtue, and like *Love*, is among the most common words used in the Holy Bible, as for that matter, in all of the holy writings of all the religions. There are more than one hundred references to forgiveness in the Bible. Every one of them specifically and unequivocally directs us *to forgive our transgressors as we are forgiven our own wrongdoings*. In no instance are any conditions specified and in all instances we are expected to willingly and unconditionally forgive others. Without this condition, we cannot be expected, nor are we able to receive forgiveness for ourselves from God or man.

For as long as man has been in existence, the inability or the refusal to provide or accept forgiveness has been the cause of more suffering, turmoil and soul destruction than any other single factor in human relationship. This has been the cause of more animosity and hate among the peoples and nations of the world and has given rise to more conflicts and wars than any other factor in human behavior. The history of the world is replete with examples of unnecessary conflicts and suffering resulting from unwillingness to forgive or even to understand other people's actions.

Forgiveness is described by Psychologists as a *Primary Principle in human behavior*, a state of resolution which serves to restore and maintain a balance in human response and behavior. It is a quality by which a person ceases to feel further resentment against another for a wrong committed against him. To forgive means to give up, stop resenting or pardon someone for an offense, real or imagined, committed. That action will restore the previous balance and trust that existed. It is impossible, both psychologically and physically, to maintain any form of equilibrium when one remains encumbered by a state of unresolved emotion. It inevitably creates internal forces which tend to induce variations in subsequent behavior with ultimate deterioration in outcome. In the end, irrespective of whether one feels justified or not, everyone loses by its continuation.

The act of forgiving another begins with the forgiving of oneself. It is impossible to forgive others of any transgression if we are not able to deal with our own internal conflicts. People involved in conflict resolution will invariably attest that before any resolution can take place the individuals must be encouraged to undergo their own self evaluation and resolve their conflicts before moving forward. This is not difficult to understand since in the great majority of cases the basic reason for the conflict itself most often results from or is exaggerated by the individual's preconceived make-up. This gives truth to the statement that *"it is not what you do, but what I think you do, that creates the difference"*.

It is the very act of granting forgiveness that allows us to grow in strength, confidence and maturity. In fact it is a lot easier to remain in a negative state withholding forgiveness, blaming the other person or circumstance, than to face up to the reality that you may be responsible, if only in part, for the continuation of the status quo. It is this fundamental resistance to admit our own weakness that forces us to hold on to resentment and hurt, and reinforces our determination against change. Because change means admission of personal responsibility, something most people are reluctant to do.

Over and over during my many years of practice I have seen dramatic changes following successful resolution that I am convinced that it is the rule rather than the exception. I refer to the amazing transformation which invariably occurs after a situation is successfully resolved. Understanding returns with both parties as does forgiveness of one another. The aura of relief and joy is palpable to all and the sense of peace and happiness, overwhelming. The impact is so powerful at times that I am convinced that even the heavens celebrate these moments.

If only people will realize that the act of not forgiving is a disease which inevitably affects the mind and body of all concerned, and that to forgive is therapeutic, as it is blessed. The relief that results is very palpable and very personal. Despite this many people will not let go, but will continue to travel on that lonely road. They are forever prisoners of their own making even as it destroys them and their relationships. In this context I am reminded of the very brief and poignant quotation, written by renowned American author and theologian *Lewis B. Smedes*, which speaks so eloquently on the true effect of forgiving to the forgiver:

> *"To forgive is to set a prisoner free,*
> *and discover the prisoner was you".*

But to me, perhaps the best advice anyone could pass on to those people suffering from the pains of *"forgivelessness"* are the words of the Holy Bible contained in *Ephesians 4:31-32:*

> *"Let all bitterness, wrath, anger, clamor, and evil speaking*
> *be put away from you together with all malice.*
> *And be kind to one another, tender hearted, forgiving one another,*
> *even as God in Christ forgave you".*

And forgive us our debts,
As we forgive our debtors.
.....Matthew 6: 9

For if you forgive men their trespasses,
your heavenly Father will also forgive you.
But if you do not forgive men their trespasses,
neither will your Father forgive your trespasses.
.....Matthew 6:14-15

Forgive us our sins, for we also forgive everyone who sins against us.
.....Luke 11: 4

"If we really want to love we must learn how to forgive"
......Mother Teresa

When asked by an offender for forgiveness,
one should forgive with a sincere mind and a willing spirit
. . . forgiveness is natural to the seed of Israel.
.....Mishneh Torah

He who Forgives, and is reconciled unto his enemy,
shall receive his reward from God.
.......Holy Koran

In the law of Karma, we realize that it is not a matter of seeking
revenge but of practicing forgiveness,
......Buddhist Teaching

Righteousness is the one highest good;
Forgiveness is the one supreme peace;
.....Hindu Teaching

The weak can never forgive.
Forgiveness is the attribute of the strong.
.......Mohandas Gandhi

Forgive all who have offended you, not for them, but for yourself.
.......Harriet Nelson

He who cannot forgive breaks the bridge over
which he himself must pass.
........George Herbert

Never does the human soul appear so strong
as when it foregoes revenge,
and dares forgive an injury.
.... H. Chapin

Without forgiveness, life is governed by
an endless cycle of resentment and retaliation.
........Roberto Assagioli

Forgiveness is not an occasional act,
It is a permanent attitude.
......Martin Luther King, Jr,

Life with Phobia

"My mind is on a constant roller coaster ride. I can never quiet my thoughts. These thoughts are so repulsive to me that I go through intense feelings of anxiety and panic. When these thoughts begin, I feel like the world is closing in around me. My body begins to shake and my nerves become raw. I get instantly dizzy and feel like I could faint at any moment"

These words expressed to me by a patient at 4.00am shortly after she awoke from a deep sleep, underlines the intense urgency and fear experienced at the time. The patient was describing an *Acute Phobic Reaction*, often called a *Panic Attack,* one of the most common forms of severe anxiety disorders.

The word "Phobia" is a term used to describe a persistent, irrational fear that causes a person to feel intense anxieties. It affects people of all ages and all intellectual, income and social levels. It has no respect of geographic or racial differences. They are the most common psychiatric illness among women of all ages and the second commonest among adult men.

Although they may be associated with global triggers, they are most often identified with a single one or group of triggers which appear to be consistently present. Sometimes the trigger may be easily identified such as heights, enclosed spaces, darkness or specific insects or animals, but most of the time it is not easily identified because of intense emotional involvement. In fact these triggers may arise from any aspect of human behavior or association and more than 100 have been identified and named.

The response may vary widely ranging from a mild symptom or two easily managed and not causing significant inconvenience, to a full blown panic attack with severe manifestations such as restlessness, shortness of breath, irregular heartbeats, profuse sweating and uncontrollable shaking. In extreme cases these symptoms can immobilize the patient to such an extent that they become prisoners in their homes.

A variety of theories have been offered by Psychologists to explain the causes of phobias, but it is generally accepted that they result from a complex mixture of internal predispositions, external experiences on underlying biological and psychological factors. In any single case a diagnosis is made after a review of the patient's social, environmental, family and life history, together with heredity, genetic and biochemical consideration. All of these may have significant roles in the development and continuation of the disorder and must be considered when formulating a treatment plan.

Because of the patient's underlying fears and anxieties, the management of these disorders is often more difficult than they ought to be. Since the symptoms are invariably precipitated by triggers which may be real, anticipated or imagined, clearly treatment, to be successful, must be directed at the identification and neutralization of all. To this end, a large variety of techniques and programs have been developed, including desensitization and/or exposure therapy, behavior modification, psychotherapy, hypnosis and relaxation therapy. In addition, a large variety of drugs are available including both psychotropic drugs such as tranquilizers and antidepressants, and drugs designed to correct the brain chemistry such as beta-blockers.

In the end however, real success can only be achieved by working with the patient to develop insight and understanding of the mechanisms that gave rise to the symptoms. For it is only by identifying the causative factors can you hope to neutralize and replace them. This requires patience, understanding and a willingness to learn, coupled with the support of a competent therapist with whom a good rapport is essential. There are several very good programs available but these are only successful if the patients is motivated enough to want to change their lives.

Unfortunately, too often we tend to deal with the situation by providing symptomatic relief. We are quick to offer tranquilizers and sedatives to relieve the immediate symptoms. By doing this, we in fact only compound the issue. Because of the nature of the condition and the ease of developing dependency, medications should be used with caution and for short periods, and never ever given on an "as needed" basis.

Life's Integrity

*Integrity is not a conditional word. It doesn't blow in the wind or
change with the weather. It is your inner image of yourself,
and if you look in there and see a man who won't cheat,
then you know he never will."*

This quotation, written by John D. MacDonald the prolific American
author, very clearly defines the true meaning of Integrity. To me,
integrity goes hand-in-hand with character and honesty. Together they make
up the inner sense of "wholeness" consistent with moral soundness in thought
and action. To be genuine and consistent, integrity must possess a continuous
and unbroken completeness or totality with nothing wanting or missing. It is
an all or none possession and cannot be used as a tool of convenience. *-That is
manipulation.*

In everyday life, integrity can be seen in every aspect of living. It is that
inner drive that compels you to do the right thing at all cost. It forces you do
the petty or unpopular things, even when no one was looking and no one cared,
because it is just the right thing to do. It is also the feeling of satisfaction you
experience after completing the right task, even though this may have been to
your disadvantage. It is also, knowing that although doing the right thing may be
tough and demanding, in the end, only good feelings, not guilt or regret, results
from it. It is the having to stand against your friends and associates when their
actions compromise what you know is right and appropriate. It often makes you
very unpopular and sometimes leads to isolation and criticism, but this a the
price you must be prepared to pay.

But integrity, when used effectively, must be tempered with good sense and fairness. At all times, it must be free of the blind and indiscriminate rage of the fanatic, whose actions are not based on reason or good sense, but rather on irrational enthusiasm or uncritical zeal. Where the fanatic's actions are invariably selfish and contrary to the well being of the general society, the exact opposite is seen in an environment where integrity is dominant. If more people in this world were to practice genuine integrity, the world would be a better and safer place. Unfortunately today's society as a whole, has sacrificed its principles of integrity on the altar of convenience and individual domination. As a result we are faced with a world consumed with hate and rage and anger and distrust, where the only solution seems to be in mutual suspicion and destruction. Where even among the leaders of the nations, integrity is as rare as a snow storm in July and where lying and cheating and deceit is the norm.

Despite this, there is no shortage of people of integrity in the world. Each one of us can readily identify people whose behavior has engendered profound respect and admiration. They come from all sections of the society irrespective of age, sex, race or levels of education. It must first begin with each one of us and with our relationship with the people around us, our family, our friends, our neighbors and others close to us. We must commit to live in truth in the way we think, we act and live and to everyone in our life. It means establishing standards and refusing to compromise even if it affects us negatively. It means that you avoid any situation where the behavior of others creates conflict, or agree to act in any way that is not true and correct. It means not tolerating any behavior that is not consistent with the highest levels and being willing to move away rather than continue and compromise.

A life without integrity is a life of never ending turmoil. actions are inconsistent and behavior unpredictable. Where you are behaving and saying one thing on the outside while feeling and believing something quite different on the inside. This is a formula for emotional volatility and distress. Yet many knowingly choose to continue to live under this cloud of negativity so that they could conform with and please the majority. This indeed is the real curse of our civilization.

In the final analysis, *Alan K. Simpson*, the American politician from Wyoming was very correct when he adapted a very popular saying while discussing the subject of integrity:

"If you have Integrity, nothing else matters.
If you don't have Integrity, nothing else matters".

The time is always right, to do what is right.
...Martin Luther King, Jr.

To know what is right and not do it,
Is the worst cowardice,
....Confucius

Laws control the lesser man.
Integrity controls the greater one.
Chinese Proverb

A life lived with Integrity - even if it lacks the trappings of fame and fortune, is a shinning star in whose light others may follow in the years to come.
......Denis Waitley

Integrity is the essence of everything successful.
.......R. Buckminster Fuller

If everyone were clothed with Integrity;
If every heart were just, frank, kindly;
then the other virtues would be well-nigh useless.
........Jean Baptiste Molière

One of the truest tests of Integrity
is its blunt refusal to be compromised.
.......Chinua Achebe

Nothing so completely baffles one who is full of trick and
duplicity himself,
than straightforward and simple Integrity in another.
.......Charles Caleb Colton

Personal Values

Personal Values are the anchor that holds us steady in all conditions. And the glue that binds us together.

They are the arbiters of right and wrong and are responsible for the moral qualities that make up our characters and determine our identities.

They provide us with the equipment to cope with our challenges and the strength to continue onward.

The successes or failures in our life are directly related to the strengths or weaknesses of our values and on nothing else.

Life with Honesty

"*And my Honesty will testify for me in the future.*"

....GENESIS 30:33

We have all grown up hearing the term *"honesty is the best policy"* so very often at home, in school, on the sports field and in church that we take it for granted and very rarely do we question its validity or necessity. Honesty, the quality of being honest, is a basic value of human behavior which can be defined in variety of ways. In terms of human communication, people are considered to be honest when they tell the truth to the best of their knowledge, or do not withhold or alter what they know or think. In respect of behavior, honesty refers to doing the right thing or abstaining from wrong or unacceptable actions, such as stealing or cheating. In essence, honesty incorporates the concepts of truthfulness and reliability. It is an integral part all human thought, words, actions and relationships.

Dr. Hal Urban, the celebrated teacher and author, wrote in his book, "*Life's Greatest Lessons*":

"*You'll never be truly successful unless everything you do,
is under-girded with honesty and integrity*"

This statement perfectly encapsulates the fundamental ingredient for the successful conduct of anyone of us. Combined with Integrity, every aspect on life becomes fulfilling and rewarding. Not because other people expect you to do so, but for your own self. Without the intrinsic platform of honesty, any action taken will be robbed of the fundamental quality of reliability. This is likely to produce a sense of doubt, leading inevitably to mistakes. Shakespeare in *Hamlet* accurately referred to this situation when he cautioned:

> *"To thine own self be true,*
> *and it must follow, as the night the day,*
> *Thou canst not then be false to any man".*

It is unfortunate that we live in a world where honesty is valued and yet shunned at the same time. We expect people to be honest in their dealings with us yet we watch and applaud television shows and movies that promote and encourage lying and deceitfulness. Without thinking, we teach our children that dishonesty is acceptable, when we ask our children to tell the caller on the telephone we are not home, or when we refuse invitations and pretend we are busy. These are lessons in deceit and in lying. On the one hand, we admonish our children for telling lies and yet we have no hesitation to lying when it suits us. Children learn by observing us and we should not be surprised that the more we expose them to a world that tolerates deceit, the more honesty will disappear from the hearts of the next generation.

But honesty is not always as easy or as practical to maintain. Sometimes by being honest, we risk harm to ourselves or equally, may cause harm to others, neither of which we might find to be acceptable. There are times when the truth if exposed, may lead to unintended results which may give rise to regret. In such situations, for example, when knowledge given in secret may cause serious consequences if released, we must rely on our integrity to counsel us in keeping our secret in order to spare the feelings of others.

Often the manipulation of honesty may be dictated by self-interest and self-protection, to ensure personal gain at the expense of others. In such situations unless tempered by a sound integrity these are likely to result in fake or immoral outcomes. These are probably one of the commonest actions seen in society and one that causes much unnecessary pain. It is no surprise therefore that genuine honesty, tempered by integrity, is considered to be a virtue, equated to dignity and to honor.

In the end, the true measure of a successful person is not in the power he possesses, nor in the wealth he accumulated nor even his social stature, but in his good name and in his honesty. George Washington summarized this very correctly when he wrote:

I hope I shall always possess firmness and virtue enough,
to maintain what I consider the most enviable of all titles;
-The character of an Honest Man."

A Honest man's word is as good as his bond.
.......CervantesWhere is there dignity unless there is Honesty?
........Cicero

Every man has his fault, and Honesty is his.
......William Shakespeare

The elegance of Honesty needs no adornment.
.......Merry Browne

Dare to be Honest and fear no labor.
.......Robert Burns

To make your children capable of Honesty,
is the beginning of education.
.......John Ruskin

I have found that being Honest is the best technique I can use.
Right up front, tell people what you're trying to accomplish,
and what you're willing to sacrifice to accomplish it.
.... Lee Iacocca

Honesty is as rare as a man without self-pity.
.... Stephen Vincent Benet

The measure of life is not strength, but Honesty.
.......John Lyle

Lands mortgaged may return, and more esteemed,
But Honesty once pawned, is never redeemed.
.......Thomas Middleton

An Honest man's the noblest work of God.
.......Alexander Pope

There is no twilight zone of Honesty in business.
A thing is right or it's wrong. It's black or it's white.
.......John F. Dodge

The elegance of Honesty needs no adornment.
.......Merry Browne

Life with Quality

"Quality is never an accident; it is always the result of high intention, sincere effort, intelligent direction and skillful execution; It represents the wisest choice of many alternatives. It also marks the search for an ideal, after necessity has been satisfied and mere usefulness achieved"

The above quotation is generally ascribed to *PFC. William A. Foster,* a United States Marine who received the Medal of Honor and the Purple Heart for his *"conspicuous gallantry and intrepidity at the risk of his life above and beyond the call of duty"* in 1945, during Battle of Okinawa in World War II. It describes in a very simple, but complete way, the true meaning of Quality.

The definition of Quality is never precise. It is multi-faceted and most often based on such factors as personal values, context, previous experience, and the expectations of the observer. The most dominant characteristic is its complexity. It is used in so many different situations that its actual definition is unique to the individual and to how he chooses to frame it. If a group of people were asked to define the term, they are more likely to give completely different answers, and less likely to exhibit unanimous agreement.

In whatever context however, the term Quality refers to that inherent distinguishing property or characteristic that can be easily recognized, if not clearly understood. It is that personal trait, or character, or appearance, or action that identifies it as unique and special, and worthy of notice. Quality, whether it relates to a person, an object, an action or a thought will always stand out when measured against the norm. It is an action worthy of respect and emulation in every aspect of life. Without its presence, life will quickly deteriorate into mundane mediocrity.

Each individual functions under his own personal standards and his own expectations. Contrary to the generally accepted view, quality is not achieved by following a standard set of rules or by copying a successful program. Quality is about commitment and effort and dedication to a personal ideal, and a willingness to act according to these ideals irrespective of the prevailing norms. Quality is recognizable, consistent and reproducible. To be successful it requires a degree of commitment and confidence in any action contemplated. Hence, giving rise to often repeated and quite appropriate statement:

> *"I don't know how to describe it,*
> *but I know it when I see it"*

All of us in our day-to-day lives inevitably search out and try to adopt the quality actions of others and incorporate them into our own. When faced with situations needing resolution, we will subconsciously look for solutions from others whom we respect, who we place in the "quality bracket." These people, by their impact upon us, have earned our respect and our recognition. They readily stand out and we usually have no difficulty in identifying them.

Over the years, in my own life, like no doubt in so many others, I have been exposed to a multitude of quality encounters, whether they are people, events or situations that have profoundly impacted me. In one way or another, these experiences have served to mould me into the person I am today. Like my Science teacher who taught me the meaning of dedication, or my Uncle, who taught me the principles of honor and justice, or my Priest, from whom I learnt the meaning God's love to all, or the Gentle woman who showed me the beauty of having total faith even in times of turmoil, or the Neighbor whose life was devoid of envy or the Business man who was committed to the welfare of his workers at all cost, or my Father whose life was committed to the welfare of his family and his good name. These are all quality people whose lives were examples of genuine quality living.

This is but a minute list of all the quality encounters that have served to influence me and to instill a desire to grow and improve. Nothing in our lives can serve as effectively as the direct and indirect influence of quality on our progress, and nothing is more damaging than our resistance or rejection of the quality people or events in our lives. If we should remember anything we should remember that nothing is more important to our living than to regularly search out and learn from quality opportunities around us.

In the end, I can not do any better than to draw your attention to Robert Louis Stevenson, the celebrated 19th century Scottish author, poet and essayist who described the true impact of Quality in our lives in the following way:

> *"We must accept life for what it actually is. A challenge to our qualitywithout which we would never know of what stuff we are made of or grow to our full stature."*

I realized that quality is not about using a particular method,
or following some canned program.
Quality is about commitment and communication.
......James H. Burrill

Quality is everyone's responsibility.
.........W. Edwards Deming

Quality is not an act, it is a habit.
.... Aristotle

Associate yourself with men of good Quality,
if you esteem your own reputation;
It is better be alone than in bad company.
.......George Washington

It is the Quality of our work which will please God
...... and it is not the quantity.
...Mohandas Gandhi

Quality begins on the inside, and then works its way out.
...... Bob Moawad

Quality means doing it right when no one is looking
.......Henry Ford

The Quality, not the longevity, of one's life is what is important.
........Martin Luther King Jr

Living with Charity
A Personal View

> "And now abideth Faith, Hope, Charity, these three;
> But the greatest of these is Charity."
>
> ......I CORINTHIANS 13:13

Charity has existed for as long as man has inhabited this world. In the simplest terms it means being aware and caring towards others in need. It exists, to a greater or lesser extent, among all peoples and religions, where the provision of alms is embedded in the teachings and practices. It is most extensively developed in the "Abrahamic" religions of Christianity, Judaism and Islam, where it constitutes a major foundation of belief that *"its practice glorifies and pleases God."* The Holy Bible, both the Old and New Testaments, and the Talmud contain an abundance of references attesting to the cardinal demand for *"Obedience to God and care of the needy."* Islam is equally referenced. In the Koran, charity is referred to as *"Zakat"* and is considered to be the third of the five pillars on which the Muslim faith is based.

To the great majority of people, the concept of charity is deeply engrained as an action that should be admired, respected and emulated and that the charitable practitioner deserves special acknowledgement and recognition for the actions. To some extent, successful people are measured by their attitude in fostering and encouraging charity to others. A society that promotes and facilitates charity to the needy by supporting organizations or opportunities for its members to assist in caring and alleviating the needs of the less fortunate is always held in higher regard.

Religious organizations are very often assessed by the extent to which they encourage charitable activity among their followers. Charitable actions take many forms and have many reasons but in all cases it can only be genuine if the real intention is helping the needy and disenfranchised. So often these actions are taken that appear to be charitably motivated but in fact are done for personal aggrandizement or gain. This is always unfortunate and should be condemned at all times.

In my experience there is a very strong underlying emotional component associated with giving that reflects the true personality of the giver and confirms the old adage, *"You can always tell a man by how he gives."* Take for example the case of two of the world's richest men, Bill Gates and Warren Buffett, who recently announced their intention to pledge much of their own wealth to charitable causes designed to improve the health and welfare of people around the world, beginning during their lifetime and continuing on. This decision speaks volumes to the character of these men who, on the one hand, are recognized as strong-willed, determined and uncompromising businessmen who will spare nothing to dominate and succeed in the business world, and yet be sensitive enough to recognize the overwhelming good that can be achieved in the welfare of millions of the less fortunate of the world. The difference is even more commendable when this action is compared to those of so many other people who choose to spend their riches on collecting multimillion dollar homes and planes and boats and cars and "wives", while totally ignoring the rest of the world. The world is full of these people and their names and pictures are prominently displayed in every form of public media and sadly, with public acceptance and adoration.

But men like Gates and Buffett are not unique. They have always been around in every generation as well-meaning philanthropists motivated to give back some of their success by improving the lot of those people in need. The great industrialist, Andrew Carnegie, accepted by many as the first of the great modern philanthropists, in his essay entitled *The Gospel of Wealth,* recorded his concept *"that rich men are trustees of their wealth and should administer it for the good of the public".* He spent his life in this pursuit of providing educational opportunities, libraries, schools and universities and in the search for international peace.

No surprise that names like Carnegie, Gates and Buffett will live on in the hearts and minds of people the world over, long after the names of so many of their equally successful peers, with their wealth and accompanying "bling", have been buried into oblivion by the sands of time. The world is full of these people who chose to give of themselves and their possessions to help others. They do it voluntarily, often at great personal inconvenience and discomfort, because of a profound desire to give back. I personally hold these people in highest esteem for in my mind. They live the true Christian ideals. Consider the very successful Irish entertainer, Bono (Paul Hewson), who has spent his professional life parlaying his fame into a universal campaign to persuade governments worldwide to improve the humanitarian needs of their people. He is but one of the many examples of successful individuals who give their names and their efforts to benefit others. They all deserve our deepfelt gratitude and our respect. Especially when compared with their equally successful "material" peers who prefer to be seen in the latest issues of *People Magazine* or *Vanity Fair,* or worse than this, spend their time in a *Drunken or Drug induced stupor.*

But charity is not solely restricted to successful and well motivated businessmen and is most certainly not reserved to a special group. Every moment of every day in every corner of the world, a charitable event unfurls and someone gives while another benefits. All of these are as important as the organized and supervised programs run by an organization. Real charity begins at home, in our families, in our personal contacts, in our neighborhood and in each life. It is a sacred duty of parents to teach by word and by example, the true value of charity. To me, giving charity however desirable, is a very personal undertaking and reflects the true character of the individual and is much more related to *intent* rather than *content.* In this context, I am reminded of the comment of Jesus Christ, contained in the Holy Scripture in *Luke 21:1-4:*

> *"He looked up and saw the rich putting their gifts into the treasury;*
> *and he saw a poor widow put in two copper coins, and he said,*
> *"Truly I tell you, this poor widow has put in more than all of them; for*
> *they all contributed out of their abundance, but she out of her poverty*
> *put in all the living that she had."*

Ask yourself, how much better this world would be if each one of us took the time to show love and caring to a fellow human being who needed that one-on-one contact. As the late Louis Armstrong, one of the greatest entertainers the world has ever seen, was so fond of saying:

"What a wonderful world this will be".

Charity suffers long, and is kind; Charity envies not;
Charity vaults not itself, is not puffed up.
. . . . I Corinthians 13:4

Charity, well directed, should begin at home.
. . . . . .Joaquin Miller

Charity and personal force are the only investments worth anything.
. . . . . . Walt Whitman

The practice of Charity will bind us;
It will bind all men in one great brotherhood.
. . . . . .Conrad Hilton

Charity is a virtue of the heart, and not of the hands.
. . . . . .Joseph Addison

The smallest act of charity shall stand us in great stead.
. . . . .Francis Atterbury

True charity is spontaneous and finds its own occasion;
it is never the offspring of importunity, nor of emulation.
. . . . . .Hosea Ballou

The Charities of life are scattered everywhere;
Enameling the vales of human beings as the flowers paint the
meadows.
They are not the fruit of study, nor the privilege of refinement,
and need no trumpet in the receiver.
......Francis Beaumont

True Charity, a plant divinely nursed.
.....William Cowper

The highest exercise of Charity is charity towards the uncharitable.
.....Joseph Stevens Buckminster

Life with Wealth

"Money shouts, Wealth whispers".

*T*he above statement was recently made by a good friend and colleague, during a discussion on the achievement and behavior of people of wealth. In a simple, but truly profound way, it describes the fundamental differences among people who have successfully accumulated large sums of money. One only has to compare the obscene image of the very successful artists or sports personalities whose multimillion dollar earnings are flouted in the form of extravagant jewelry, mansions with gold plated ceilings and extra-ordinary vehicles that go nowhere, to that of Warren Buffett, one of the most successful entrepreneurs ever, who while being content to live in the same home and drive the same old car, chose to donate more than 80% of his estate to charitable causes.

Unfortunately, in the United States more than in any of the other western industrial democracies, there is an outrageous and perhaps, an unconscionable, disparity in the acquisition and distribution of wealth. This has led to the present lopsided distribution where the top 1% of households own almost 50% of privately held wealth, and more than 80% of the population share less than 15%.

It would appear that to many that the real description of the "American dream" is the accumulation of wealth without regard to social justice or responsibility. A very good example of this immoral greed was seen in the follow-up to the recent collapse of the *American International Group*. After receiving more than $170 billion in taxpayer bailout money from the Treasury and Federal Reserve to save them from certain bankruptcy, they promptly proceeded with plans to pay about $165 million in bonuses to the executives in the same business unit that brought the company to the brink of collapse last year, without any regard to the thousands of people who lost their homes and livelihood.

Andrew Carnegie, the great American industrialist, in his essay, *Gospel of Wealth* (1889), was among the first to recognize the impact of modern civilization and the resulting disparity in conditions resulting from industrialization. He expressed his concerns thus:

> *"The problem of our age is the proper administration of wealth,*
> *so that the ties of brotherhood may still bind together the rich and poor*
> *in harmonious relationship."*

The central core of his thesis was that the wealthy entrepreneur must accept the responsibility of distributing his fortune in a way that will be put to good use, and not wasted on frivolous over-indulgence. He further suggested that the very existence of poverty in a capitalistic society could be completely eliminated by wealthy philanthropic men who are merely trustees of their wealth and are duty-bound to administer it for the good of the people.

Men like Buffett and Carnegie deserve our genuine respect and recognition. They are people who are endowed with the special gift for success and have worked to achieve the rewards of this gift, but have never lost sight of its true meaning. To them, the reward is not in the accumulation of wealth, but in the recognition and expression of its meaningful redistribution. They do not need to advertise their wealth, their words and deeds will speak loudly for them. -Their wealth merely whispers.

However, for each one of these men, there are many others who by reason of luck, or ability, or inheritance or worse of all, by deception, have acquired large fortunes and influence. They are easily recognized, not by their good deeds or words, but by the noise they make to advertise themselves and their importance. You know them by the mansions they own, or the yachts and airplanes and automobiles they acquire, but certainly not by their concern for their environment or their less fortunate brothers. They have no hesitation in underwriting the cost of transporting the complete list of guests, entertainers and food to Morocco to celebrate a birthday party by Ken Lay of the Enron scandal, while systematically cheating thousands of investors.

Or the entertainers who have so far been unable to find a home to suit them so they sign a lease to rent a home for the obscene figure of $150,000.00 per month. These people are driven by an all-consuming greed completely devoid of any sense of caring for the less fortunate. -They use their wealth to shout out their importance.

In the final analysis, the names of these people will never live on, except possibly as a footnote in history. But the name of Carnegie continues to flourish in every school and every library because of the contributions made by his foundation. And Warren Buffett's support of a myriad of charitable organizations has achieved great success in the welfare of people and countries all over the world. These people learnt early on in their careers that the wealth they accumulate is always transient and only their name can live on. As Benjamin Franklin often reminded us:

"If your riches are yours, why can't you take them with you to the other world?"

Or as Billy Graham, one of the greatest living evangelists is fond of asking us:

"Have you ever seen a U-haul following a Hearse?"

Ill-gotten treasures are of no value,
but righteousness delivers from death.
......Proverbs 10:2

Wealth is the product of man's capacity to think.
........Ayn Rand

Though I am grateful for the blessings of wealth,
it hasn't changed who I am.
My feet are still on the ground. I'm just wearing better shoes.
.......Oprah Winfrey

Wealth is the slave of a wise man but the master of a fool.
.......Seneca

The real source of wealth and capital in this new era is not material
things.
it is the human mind, the human spirit, the human imagination,
and our faith in the future.
.......Steve Forbes

Wealth is not in making money but in making the man, while he is
making the money.
........John Wicker

Prefer loss to the wealth of dishonest gain;
The former vexes you for a time;
The latter will bring you lasting remorse
......Chilo

Money only appeals to selfishness,
and always tempts its owners irresistibly to abuse it
......Albert Einstein

Riches either serve or govern the possessor.
........Horace

Common sense among men of fortune is rare.
........Juvenal

Those who thank God much are the truly wealthy.
So our inner happiness depends not on what we experience,
but on the degree of our gratitude to God, whatever the experience.
......Albert Schweitzer

The Indispensable Man

*S*ometime ago I came across an interesting poem entitled *"The Indispensable Man"*. It was written and published in 1959 by the award winning poet and author, *Saxon Nadine White Kessinger*, of Idaho, who recently died at age 88 years. Its impact on me was profound and lasting. In a simple, precise and very effective manner she presented a very convincing argument against thinking anyone is indispensable, and laid to rest the very popular and universally held notion that some of us are irreplaceable and that what we do, or say or think will have a lasting and indelible effect on this world and on the people who inhabit it. The last verse summarized her thoughts:

> *"The moral of this quaint example,*
> *Is to do just the best that you can,*
> *Be proud of yourself but remember,*
> *There's no indispensable man."*

There is a natural tendency for us to think that we are indispensable and to believe that without us, life will not be the same. To some extent this might well be true, especially in regards to our intimate world and our friends and family. It could be argued that it serves the very important role of providing an impetus for our self-growth and our ego, and a sense of comfort and security in living and planning. To some people, it is considered to be the most important force in the initiation and continuation of any drive or ambition we possess, and in providing a meaning for living. They argue that it is only when individuals begin to think they are indispensable, that they develop a compulsive and determined temperament to achieve, because they believe that their action will have impact on others. The poem however left no doubt that our actions, however impressive at the time, by and large will leave little long term impact.

The world's history books are filled with accounts of people whose lives and actions have made them feel, or cause others to believe, that they were "indispensable". Throughout the ages most, if not all, the great leaders have at some time or other felt that they were indispensable, and that their people will suffer without them. But the real truth is that despite all of the power or achievements they amassed in life, they become a memory and a reference after death. Inevitably life continues, others take over, and in time much of the work achieved is undone and replaced or modified. Charles De Gaulle, the great French General, Statesman, Founder and President of the Fifth French Republic, credited for leading the French resistance against the German forces during the 2nd World War, was precise and accurate when he replied, in response to being described as being indispensable to the nation:

"The Cemeteries of the world are full of indispensable men."

In every generation, in every community and every country throughout the world, men and women have appeared and have achieved such outstanding results as to earn them the label of indispensability. These special and unique people, by virtue of their strong personality, magnetic force, deep commitment or inner charisma are able to motivate and impress others to do and to achieve levels far above their expectation. George Washington, the founding father of the American Republic, Abraham Lincoln, the architect of the modern United States and Martin Luther King Jr., the great civil rights leader, are examples of great leaders whose actions earned the status of indispensability. Each one of these people earned the reputation by the strength of their commitment to the cause, their leadership performance and the reaction of the people they served. They certainly deserve the respect and approval for their effort in making their world a better place during their lifetime. But these people have all moved on and the work they started has continued on without them, proving that while they may not be forgotten, they are certainly not indispensable.

Ms. Kessinger however in her poem makes the case that we devote our efforts to doing the best we can without trying to prove that we are indispensable. By doing this we will succeed in developing a healthy, balanced sense of ourselves without any need to impress anyone. As I see it, this is a very realistic and reasonable approach and one which should be used more often. Doing what you do to the best of your ability will not only benefit others but ensures your own personal satisfaction, without concern to its long term survival.

We will all do well to remember this as we travel along the road of life. How ever much we achieve or however much we impress others concerning our abilities or successes, in the end we are not, nor will we ever be indispensable. In this respect, I can do no better than to repeat the excellent advice of St. Paul to the Romans contained in his letter to them *(Romans 12:3)*:

> *"For I say, through the grace given unto me, to every man that is among you, not to think of himself more highly than he ought to think;*
> *But to think soberly, according as God hath dealt to every man the measure of faith."*

Life and the Pursuit of Happiness

"Remember the five simple rules to Happiness;
-Free your heart from hatred, Free your mind from worries,
Live simply, give more and expect less."

The above advice by an unknown author is to my mind, the most comprehensive and eloquent description for happiness I have ever encountered.
By its simplicity and clarity, it underlines, in dramatic effect, the necessary
steps needed to achieve the full rewards of a happy life. Happiness is never
ever an entitlement. It is never automatic nor is it ever inherited or passed on.
The 14th Dalai Lama, *Tenzin Gyatso*, in a discussion with students at the Florida
International University expressed this concept in the following terms:

"Happiness is not something ready made.
It comes from your own actions."

In his book entitled *"The Art of Happiness"*, published in 1998, his Holiness further elaborated his vision in these words:

"I believe that the very purpose of our life is to seek happiness. -That is
clear. Whether one believes in religion or not, whether one believes in
this religion or that religion, We all are seeking something better in life.
So, I think, the very motion of our life is towards happiness."

In all his discussions the Dalai advocates that the aim of successful life is
not in the acquisition of material fame and fortune, or even in the public

recognition of these acquisitions, but rather in the degree of pleasure and happiness we are able to achieve along the way. He stressed that this right of happiness and the ability to find it, is available to everyone who is willing to make the effort to do what is necessary to achieve it. He went further to identify steps that we must all follow in our pursuit of personal happiness. These include:

-*Establishing the right mental attitude and expectations.*
-*Achieving the correct discipline and calmness of mind.*
-*Controlling emotions, encouraging positive thoughts and suppressing negative ones.*
-*Recognizing and cultivating good habits and removing bad ones.*
-*Learning from our failures, recognizing that suffering is the opposite of happiness.*
-*Identifying and welcoming positive changes and removing older, un-productive ones.*
-*Developing long-lasting and deep-rooted relationships based on truth, honesty and respect.*

The late *Sai Baba,* the renowned Indian guru, mystic, spiritual figure and educa-tor, describes Happiness as actually being natural to human beings. He is quoted as saying that *"Since our beings consist of consciousness-energy, the nature of which is well-being, happiness is our nature. We don't need good fortune or any new circumstances to be happy, and we don't need material goods, fun activities or success or power. It's pos-sible for us just to be happy, without any reason at all, because happiness is just there, inside us, in the same way that the sky and the air are outside us."*

The well known phrase contained in *the U.S. Declaration of Independence* as an unalienable right, *"Life, Liberty and the pursuit of Happiness"* is considered to be one of the most powerful and influential statements in the English Language. It has served to underline the caliber and quality of the original framers. However, unfortunately as a society, we have failed to live up to the advice and expecta-tions of these great leaders. Instead of choosing the path to happiness as one that encompasses a meaningful life, utilizing your strengths and abilities in assisting others, and living with purpose and compassion, we chose to measure our happiness by our conquests, our successes and our material status.

It is a crying shame that our present-day society beset by useless and expensive wars, openly manipulated by greedy business leaders and governed by selfish and self-directed politicians, has lost the fundamental meaning of true happiness. Instead, we have succeeded in replacing this noble and worthy direction by one which aims at projecting the 'individual' at all cost while ignoring the legitimate needs of the less fortunate masses. We have no hesitation to glorify, to the point of adoration, the successful athlete, or entertainer, or CEO, or politician, with our praise and our money, even as they engage in a whole range of unacceptable behavior designed to provide personal pleasure and self-gratification. We have replaced the selfless happiness of *Buddha and Aristotle* with the *cult of Individualism*. We have sacrificed the true joy of *Happiness* on the altar of *Persons and Personality* as we are persuaded that "only wealth can buy happiness". And we have done all this in the name of progress!

But true happiness should not ever be measured on a yardstick of personal gain, or wealth, or popularity, nor for that matter should it be arbitrarily assumed for services rendered. Happiness is a state of being, a feeling of inner peace and acceptance that combines a whole range of attitudes and expectations. It is a very personal experience and cannot be transferred or exchanged. In this respective it is absolute, in that there can be no 'relative happiness' and you cannot share happiness of others unless it becomes assimilated within you. In every respect, I believe happiness is a choice that we each have the option to choose or to reject. It really depends on our willingness to look deeply into our own souls and to determine our own needs and purpose in life and our willingness to choose our happiness. It is sometimes difficult to understand why others can be so happy even though they function under conditions which we may regard as unacceptable. Consider the example of Mary, a middle aged lady whose life reads like a series of disasters that included a life of drug and sex abuse, rejecting religion, dealing with the occult, living in the streets and losing her only son as a young adult, until she found faith and religion. Yet if you were to meet her, you will not fail to recognize a deep seated happiness and love radiating from her and in every word she utters.

Whenever she is asked to explain why she is so happy under these difficult circumstances, she will reply:

> *"Happiness does not mean that we will never get sick or have no problems or experience no difficulties. Happiness means that when we do have them, I believe we will always find that God is at our side, holding our hands and guiding us to find a solution. To me this special relationship with God is what true happiness is all about."*

Mary clearly has learnt the real meaning of happiness and I have no doubt that her faith will continue to support her for the rest of her life.

I believe that the potential for true happiness exists within each one of us and that in the majority of cases they remain buried under the debris of modern living to such an extent as to render them unattainable. In our headlong drive to conform to, and live like our neighbors, we have lost sight of our unique ability to be ourselves, to make choices for ourselves and above all, to recognize the wisdom of the great Greek philosopher *Aristotle*, who recorded:

> *"Happiness is the meaning and the purpose of life.*
> *It is the whole aim and end of human existence."*

> *"In Buddhism, True happiness is defined as*
> <u>*Riyaku, Sesshua, and Fusha:*</u>
> -<u>*"Riyaku"*</u>: *means peace, satisfaction and joy referred as happiness.*
> -<u>*"Sesshu"*</u>: *means embraced firmly and satisfied completely.*
> -<u>*"Fusha"*</u>: *means never forsaken and changed."*
> …..*Buddhist Teaching*

> *You may traverse the world in search of happiness,*
> *when it is within the reach of every man.*
> *A contented mind confers it on all.*
> …..*Horace*

Events will take their course. It is no good of being angry at them;
He is happiest who wisely turns them to the best account.
. . . . .Euripides

The word "happiness" would lose its meaning,
if it were not balanced by sadness.
. . . . . .Carl Jung

Happiness is like a butterfly which when pursued,
is always beyond your grasp;
But if you sit down quietly may alight upon you.
. . . . . . .Nathaniel Hawthorne.

Happiness is like a kiss.
You must share it to enjoy it.
. . . .Bernard Meltzer

You cannot always have happiness,
but you can always give happiness.
. . . . . .Author Unknown

Happiness is when what you think, what you say,
and what you do are in harmony.
. . . . . . .Mohandas Gandhi

When one door of Happiness closes, another opens;
But often we look so long at the closed door,
that we do not see the one which has opened for us.
. . . . . . .Helen Keller

Learning from Experience

> *"All true learning is experience.*
> *Everything else is just information."*

hese words recorded by Albert Einstein in the 1990's during a discussion on the effect of experience in learning very effectively condenses one of the most important principles in learning. Learning is generally defined as a *"process of acquiring knowledge or skill through study, experience or teaching"*. But to me, true learning is much more complex than this. It can only be considered meaningful when it is accompanied with changes in the basic understanding and behavioral potential of the individual. It is not merely the acquisition of information but rather the assimilation of such information and its subsequent incorporation into the individual's psyche. In truth, we are what we learn. Over our lifetime I believe that the experience of Living is by far the greatest and most effective source of learning.

This fundamental fact has been universally recognized throughout the ages by the majority of the great thinkers and philosophers of all cultures. The renowned ancient Roman philosophers Pliny and Tacitus insisted that *"Experience is the most efficient teacher"*, and Julius Caesar publicly acknowledged that *"Experience is the teacher of all things."* Mahatma Gandhi went further and noted that *"knowledge gained through experience is far superior and many times more useful than bookish knowledge."*

Formal education, though extremely important in assisting us to obtain the best opportunities in our lives, is not necessarily <u>the</u> most important component. The history of the world is replete with examples of people who have become very successful in every conceivable aspect of life without ever completing their appropriate formal education. This should not be surprising since in most instances their success is based on their innate ability to maximize their life experiences. The following are some of the endless examples of people whose contributions have changed the course of history:

-*Abraham Lincoln,* considered one of the greatest U.S. Presidents, finished 1 year of formal schooling then continued his education by self-teaching to become a lawyer.

-*Andrew Jackson,* successful as a soldier, lawyer, judge and U.S. president, was essentially home-schooled, without receiving any formal school education.

-*Benjamin Franklin,* one of the greatest sons of America, a founding father of the nation, inventor, scientist, author and entrepreneur relied primarily home-schooling.

-*Christopher Columbus,* the great explorer who discovered the Americas was essentially self-taught, learning all the intricacies of sailing from experience.

-*Frank Lloyd Wright,* possibly the most famous architect of the twentieth century, never continued beyond primary school.

-*Henry Ford,* the father of the assembly line for car-making never completed high school.

-*Winston Churchill,* considered one of the greatest British statesmen, historian and artist, failed high school and never attended college. He was credited with saving Britain during WW11.

In my own lifetime many of the very successful inventors, entrepreneurs and game changers I have encountered or have read about have been high school and/or college dropouts who chose to abandon the formal programs of learning to go their own way. These include, *Bill Gates* and *Paul Allen*(microsoft), *Michael Dell* (computers), *Larry Ellison*(oracle), *Steve Jobs*(apple), *Larry Page* and *Sergio Brin*(google) and *Mark Zuckerberg*(facebook). Because of their individual and joint efforts, they have succeeded in changing the world in unimaginable ways over a period of just over a decade. In all these cases, these exceptional people chose to forego the conventional road to enrichment and trusting their instincts, go forward on their own learning as they moved on.

This does not, in my mind, argue, as many people have, for the condemnation of an organized schooling system as a primary source of education. The overwhelming majority of students require an organized, structured, orderly milieu to be able to learn and to grow. For these students it is therefore imperative that they be offered the best possible opportunity to learn and acquire knowledge. But there will always be a special group of individuals who will rise above the conventional standard and choose their own road, using nothing but experience and their innate ability as their guide.

Unfortunately the true failing of our educational systems is that they do not make allowance for the needs and variations of the individual student. They cannot provide the flexibility to allow the individual to learn from experience in the group setting of formal teaching. Instead students spend their learning years locked in a proscribed curriculum, held within boundaries laid down for the majority, which are zealously guarded under the pretext of being the only efficient way. It is no surprise therefore that the majority of students complete their education full of knowledge but unwilling to venture out and risk failure.

Within the last twenty years however the situation has been changing as educationalists search for ways to effectively incorporate experiential learning into the conventional systems. This is very definitely facilitated by the universal availability of computers, the increased use of interactive procedures by teachers and students and the rapid development of electronic based programs. This, to my mind, is clearly the direction to follow since it provides a range of opportunities to satisfy the different needs of the students and allows them to develop to their maximal potential at their own pace. All this in keeping with the famous quotation by Xun Kuang, a Chinese Confucian Philosopher who lived from 312 – 230 BC:

Tell me and I forget.
Teach me and I remember.
Involve me and I learn.

Outlook on Life

Two men look out the same prison bars;
One sees mud and the other stars.

*T*his famous quotation by Rev. Frederick Langbridge, the Irish author and novelist, precisely encapsulates the true meaning of Outlook and its subsequent effect on behavior.

The Thesaurus defines Outlook as *a habitual or characteristic mental attitude that determines how you will interpret and respond to situations*. It is a fundamental and simply uncontroversial truth that a positive outlook in life makes a world of difference on the outcome of any encounter, and equally, the wrong outlook dooms even the simplest task. Being positive and optimistic about a situation, irregardless of its complexity and difficulty, will go a long way to helping in achieving success. And by contrast, even the simplest task could have a disastrous outcome in the hands of someone who is primed to fail.

In this context I am reminded of a song made popular by Frank Sinatra in 1959 entitled, *"High Hopes"*, which was adopted and modified by John F. Kennedy in 1960 at the start of his successful presidential campaign. The song deals with a few bizarre scenarios where animals challenge and overcome impossible situations as a result of their positive outlook, such as, *an ant moving a tree*, and *a ram bringing down a dam*. It created a sensation when it was published and not only won the Academy Award for Best Song of that year, but became a standard best seller. It was used to encourage people to try harder and it certainly was very effectively used to reinforce the image of JFK as the right candidate to be president.

Acquiring the right outlook is not always easy to do. Like any other personality trait its acquisition is dependent on multiple factors including heredity, familial, environmental, educational and social exposure. The more positive environment a child is exposed to, the more encouragement he is given and the more opportunity he has to achieve success, all play major roles in reinforcing a positive outlook. By contrast, being exposed in an environment of fear and pessimism and extreme caution and timidity, will only serve to doom the child to a life committed to avoiding failure rather than achieving success.

That is a real pity, for the truth is that we can all do more and achieve more by trying to cultivate and apply a positive outlook to any situation. We cannot allow a bad experience or outcome to affect our outlook and compromise our chance of success. In fact, staying positive is not difficult to achieve, nor is it limited to a special group of people. We should all recognize that we do have the power to choose how we deal with a situation and that maintaining a positive outlook is much easier than it appears. In the end, life is what you make of it and it is up to you to decide how you deal with your problems.

Richard M. DeVos, the founder of the highly successful consumer products company, *Amway International,* described this principle quite effectively. His observation strongly deserves your sincere consideration:

"Life tends to respond to our Outlook
to shape itself to meet our Expectation."

Your Outlook upon life is largely colored by your environment.
Your whole career will be modified, shaped, molded by your surroundings,
by the character of the people with whom you come in contact every day.
……...Orison Swett Marden

The rapprochement of peoples is only possible when
differences of Outlook are respected and appreciated, rather than
feared and condemned.
……H. William Fullbright

I have treated many hundreds of patients.
Among those in the second half of life, that is to say, over 35, there
has not been one whose problem in the last resort was not that of
finding a Religious Outlook on life.
…….Carl Jung

Life with Fate

The headlines in the *Sports Section* of the morning newspaper attracted my attention. Not so much because it announced the results of yesterday's Kentucky Derby, but rather the sequence of events leading up to it. Consider the following events which took place:

-The winning jockey was offered the mount only the night before when his original mount, which was considered to be the overwhelming favorite, was scratched because of illness.

-The jockey who was originally assigned to the subsequent winner was forced to withdraw because of an injury he sustained the day before in a race won by the winning jockey.

-The Derby winner was only entered by his trainer after his stable-mate, supposedly a much better horse, was withdrawn. Also the horse had not raced for over 6 weeks and had never raced on a dirt track before, having been bred as a "grass" specialist.

-To compound the issue, the winning jockey had in past three years experienced deep disappointment when all the mounts to which he was assigned and which were all considered to be unbeatable, were scratched because of illness or injury.

After completion of the race, the newspaper sports reporter summed this whole sequence of events in the following terms:

"Perhaps the formula for victory was involving two guys with the worst luck and putting them together with a horse that has never run on dirt."

The jockey was somewhat more philosophical when he offered the following explanation:

"Things happen for a reason. I guess when it is meant for you, it is meant for you. God is in charge"

As I read this, I was reminded of a statement I had come across sometime ago as part of a contribution written by *"Rochelle"* of Austin, Texas on the *This I Believe* series conducted by National Public Radio:

"This I believe, that all things happen for a reason. I believe that we must take the bad with the good, and that sometimes unanswered prayers are God's greatest gifts, and faith is the solution to all our problems."

I believe there must be some truth in what they are saying, and although there are large numbers of very learned people who will have no hesitation to disagree, I myself will tend to favor their view. The Arabs place great store on the role of Fate (*"Naseeb"*) in all aspects of their lives. They believe there is a certain inevitability or finality in events as they unfold and that, irrespective of our plans or expectations; they will work themselves out in the end. My late mother-in-law believed very firmly in this principle and will often quote the Arabic equivalent of; *"Whatever happens will happen"*.   This fatalistic approach renders living under any circumstances acceptable since it does offer the opportunity to adapt to changing conditions.

The great German philosopher, *Friedrich Nietzsche*, a strong proponent of the influence of Fate, coined the Latin term, *Amor Fati*, which he described as *"Love Your Fate, which is in fact your life."* He expanded this view in the following quotation:

"The duty of acceptance in all that concerns the will of God, whatever it may be, was impressed upon my mind as the first and most necessary

of all duties from the time when I found it set down in Marcus Aurelius under the form of the 'amor fati' of the Stoics. I saw it as a duty we cannot fail in without dishonoring ourselves."

To him, Fate represents an attitude in which one sees everything that occurs in one's life including good and bad, joy and sorrow, success and failure or pain and suffering as a fulfillment of God's ultimate plan and therefore should be considered good and acceptable. He advocated an acceptance, without question, of the events or situations which occur during one's lifetime.

But to me Fate is not synonymous with Destiny although most people seem to think that the words are essentially interchangeable. As I see it, although Fate relates to a fixed sequence of events usually occurring outside the influence of the individual, and resulting in changes that are inevitable or unchangeable, it does not however preclude nor exclude the fact that Fate can be altered or modified by the actions of the individual. The jockey, for example, would not have been successful and therefore Fate would not have applied, had he not accepted to ride that horse in the race. *Gloria Estefan,* the successful Latin-American pop singer, expressed this accurately when she stated:

"We seal our Fate, with the choices we make."

In the final analysis, whether it was *Fate* that determined the sequence of events that led the trainer to invite the jockey to ride this particular horse to victory, or *Destiny,* that predetermined the several unique circumstances necessary to come together beforehand that ultimately resulted in success, the final victory occurred only as a result of a brilliant execution of the jockey as he guided his well-prepared horse to victory.

I can think of no better way to describe the fundamentals of this dilemma than to quote from the great *Lord Buddha,* one of the world's greatest spiritual leaders and founder of *Buddhist Religion:*

"I do not believe in a fate that falls on men, however they act;
But I do believe in a fate that falls on them, unless they act."

Men are not prisoners of fate, but only prisoners of their own minds.
.... *Franklin D. Roosevelt*

It is what a man thinks of himself that really determines his fate.
.... *Henry David Thoreau*

As punishment for my contempt for authority, fate has made me an authority myself.
.... *Albert Einstein*

Fate leads the willing, and drags along the reluctant.
.... *Seneca*

Fate is not a matter of chance; it is a matter of choice. It is not a thing to be waited for; it is a thing to be achieved.
.........*William Jennings Bryan*

When Fate hands you a lemon, try making lemonade.
....*Dale Carnegie*

There is no Fate but your own Fate.
......*Leslie Grimutter*

Control your Fate, or someone else will do so.
.....*Jack Welch*

Fate has two ways of crushing us;
-By refusing our wishes, or by fulfilling them.
.....*Henri F. Amiel*

Go with your Fate, but never beyond;
Beyond leads to dark places.
......Mary Renault

What separates the winners from the losers is how a person deals with each twist of Fate.

.....Donald Trump

Living with Destiny

"I believe in destiny. Everything in life happens for a reason. It happens simply because it is supposed to happen. Although humans are allotted the power of choice, yet the outcomes of these choices are long predetermined by some unknown force. As trivial as this ideology may seem, my personal experience has led me to become a firm believer in it."

The above quotation is taken from an essay by an author whose name I do not recall. It clearly sets out a view, widely held, that in many cases the outcomes are often predetermined, subject to an external force and beyond the voluntary control of the individual. Henry Miller, the celebrated American author, more precisely expressed this idea in this quote:

"Every man has his own Destiny, the only imperative is to follow it, to accept it; No matter where it leads him".

Yet, the completely opposite view, that Destiny is subject to our own free will and that we are responsible for who we are and what we do has very strong support. The proponents essentially reject the "pre-determined" concept, insisting that we are finally responsible for our actions. William Jennings Bryan, the great American congressman and orator, described destiny in the following manner:

"Destiny is not a matter of chance, but a matter of choice.
It is not a thing to be waited for; It is thing to be achieved".

Throughout the ages, the concept of Destiny being an occurrence subject to an "external force" has been universally accepted, and people believed and lived by the consequences. They basically attributed the source and purpose to a super-human origin and willingly accepted the consequences to the "will of God". Lord Edward Lytton, the great 19th century English poet and playwright summarized the popular view of that time thus:

> *"We are but the instrument of heaven;*
> *Our work is not Design, but Destiny".*

However during the last century, with the advancing scientific knowledge and understanding, there has been a decided shift in the Western cultures away from the idea of supernatural influence, to a more free-choice attitude. The prevailing attitude nowadays is that man is in control of his destiny and is responsible for the consequences.

This contrasts dramatically with the prevailing attitudes in Eastern and Middle Eastern cultures, where the concept of destiny as being beyond our influence, remains strongly entrenched. In the Arab culture the term *Naseeb* is used to explain outcomes beyond the individual's control. In the Asian cultures, which remain deeply rooted in the ancient customs, destiny plays a fundamental role in life based on the basic principle of *Yin and Yang*. In the ancient religions of Buddhism and Hinduism, the term *Karma* is used to explain the concept of destiny as part of the soul under the influence of the Gods.

To a significant extent, this difference explains the opposing attitudes toward life between the Eastern and Western cultures, and the willingness to accept adversity by the former without complaint. In this context I am reminded of my recent experience of a situation where a mother responded to my news of her daughter's abuse at the hands of her alcoholic husband by saying:

> *"It is God's will; -it is her Naseeb in Life".*

In contrast, the prevailing view in the Western culture is that Destiny relates to a sequence of events related to the future and although they may appear to be unalterably predetermined from an external source, however they are subject to alteration depending on the choices made by the individual. This leads on to the often conflicting argument that individuals can choose their own destiny by selecting different "paths." Others believe that throughout their lifetime, irrespective of the options exercised, the ultimate courses of action taken by the individuals will always lead to a predetermined destiny. *William Jennings Bryan,* the celebrated American politician and presidential candidate, described this situation most succinctly in this manner:

> *"Destiny is not a matter of chance;*
> *it is a matter of choice.*
> *It is not a thing to be waited for;*
> *it is a thing to be achieved."*

My own views however, based on my personal experience over the years, is that there is indeed a destiny in each one of us. Some may call it *"coincidence"*, others refer to it as *"fate"*, and the more religious will use *"divine intervention"*, but in all cases it refers to a random force, an opportunity, presenting itself in a special time and place to an individual. But that is not enough, for your destiny will only reach fruition when you are able to convert it to action. Surely we can all recognize the very many occasions where the opportunity appeared and remained unfulfilled because we were not ready or able or willing to react.

-Destiny therefore, is what you make of it!

> *"We do not do what we want,*
> *yet we are responsible for what we are;*
> *- This is fact."*
> *......Jean-Paul Satre*

Think you I bear the shear of Destiny?
Have I commandment on the pulse of life?
.....William Shakespeare

Character is Destiny.
.....Hereclitus

Your Destiny is determined by choice;
-Not by chance.
......Jean Nidetch

The chain of Destiny can only be grasped one link at a time.
.....Winston Churchill

Men heap together the mistakes of their lives;
And create a monster called Destiny.
.....John Oliver Hobbes

And when man faces Destiny;
Destiny ends, and man comes into his own.
.....Andre Malraux

One often meets his Destiny
in the road he takes to avoid it.
.....French Proverb.

The highest Destiny of man is to serve,
rather than to rule.
......Albert Einstrin

Accept the things to which fate binds you;
And love the people with whom fate brings you together.
This is your Destiny.
…..Marcus Aelius Aurelius

Our Destiny rules over us, even when we are not aware of it.
It is the future that makes laws for us today.
…..Friedrich Wilheim Nietzsche

Life with Inspiration

"It's almost magical. When inspired, time flies and productivity skyrockets".

I came across the above statement, written by an anonymous contributor, in an internet site dealing with personal experiences in the workplace. It impressed me as an excellent example of the influence of inspiration in the context of our living and working.

Inspiration is an exceedingly interesting and widely researched phenomenon that can profoundly affect human behavior in a variety of ways. It, like so many other vital phenomena in our daily lives, can only be described by its effects rather than its appearance. It is defined as *the act or power of stimulation or arousal of the mind resulting in the influencing of special or unusual activity or creativity.* It also refers to a form of *divine guidance or supernatural influence* on the mind of an individual causing or giving rise to unexpected or unpredictable outcomes. In effect the influence of inspiration is like the trigger which initiates the action. It is the spark of confidence that precipitates movement forward. it is the difference that makes the mundane become the exquisite, the stuff that allows the artist, the poet, the author or the leader to stand out and the prophet or the preacher appear as the chosen one.

But inspiration is much more than this. It is very much a human component which is present, to a smaller or larger extent, in everything we do, or think, or say. But although it may be the trigger which initiates the action, it does not provide the guarantee of successful outcome. This can only occur with the concomitant expenditure of effort by the individual. In fact life is over-run with

123

examples of brilliant inspirational ideas that have floundered and died for lack of implementation. I am reminded of the oft-quoted statement, attributed to so many authors, ancient and modern, that says:

"Success is made up of 10% Inspiration and 90% Perspiration"

In my experience both with regard to my own self, as well as in my relationship with others, I am convinced this is indeed a truism, and that in life, every form of human expression is the result of a combination of these two components. Whether the intent is to do good or evil, the impact of inspiration is equally vital. The more inspired the individual, the better or more evil he will be able to produce. Everyone will have no difficulty in identifying multiple examples of people in their own lives who have used their inspiration to produce deeds that translate to helping themselves or others or their environment, and others who have channeled their effort to illicit gain or to causing further suffering.

The great majority of successful people in the world inevitably achieved their success by virtue of their innate ability to draw upon the unique creativity conferred on them by the power of inspiration. This is the factor that allows them to stand over their peers and achieve such enviable results. The great artists and authors and thinkers and inventors and leaders have all been able to produce their work as a result of the drive initiated by their inspiration, which provided them with the foundation they needed. In the same way others have been able to use this ability to carry out the greatest injustices to humanity. Dictators like Stalin, Hitler, Castro, and the thousands of others who have appeared over the preceding centuries; Confidence tricksters like Ponzi, Madoff, and a multitude of lesser practitioners who have succeeded in cheating millions of unsuspecting people, as well as Crooks and Mobsters, who as individuals or part of an organization, have dominated the society with fear and death, have all done so as a result of their extraordinary ability to draw upon their innate inspiration and creativity.

Whether this ability is passed on from generation to generation by inheritance or by example is still hotly debated. But it should be noted that it is not unusual to see the same pattern of behavior repeating within families where members of the same family often exhibit similar behavioral and mental attitudes. In the end however, irrespective of our own personal attitudes or abilities, our lives are directly or indirectly, affected by inspiration. They can appear from any aspect of our lives or from any person, or object or any emotion. How we respond will depend to a large extent, upon our personal beliefs and attitudes. Most of us generally adopt an attitude of acceptance and are content to assign the outcome as a product of divine intervention. As the famous 16th century French apothecary, author and astronomer, *Michel de Nostradame (Nostradamus)* explained:

> *"Perfect knowledge cannot be acquired without divine inspiration;*
> *Given that all prophetic inspiration derives its initial origin from God*
> *Almighty."*

> *But there is a spirit in man:*
> *And the inspiration of the Almighty gives them understanding.*
> *......Job 32:8*

> *Action always generates inspiration.*
> *Inspiration seldom generates action.*
> *......Frank Tibolt*

> *What that man creates by means of reason will pale,*
> *before the art of inspired beings.*
> *......Pheadrus.*

> *In life you need either inspiration or desperation.*
> *.....Anthony Robbins*

> *No one was ever great without some portion of divine inspiration.*
> *....Marcus Tullius Cicero*

Inspiration comes from the Heart of Heaven to give the lift of wings,
and the breath of divine music to those of us who are earthbound.
..... Margaret Sangster

Method is much, technique is much, but inspiration is even more.
.....Benjamin Cardozo

Inspiration never arrived when you were searching for it.
.......Lisa Alther

Keep your fears to yourself, but share your inspiration with others.
.....Robert Louis Stevenson

Inspiration is a guest who does not like to visit lazy people.
......Tchaikowsky

Inspiration follows aspiration.
.....Rabindranath Tagore

Living with your Thoughts

"Carefully watch your Thoughts, for they become your Words.
Manage and watch your Words, for they will become your Actions.
Consider and judge your Actions, for they have become your Habits.
Acknowledge and watch your Habits, for they shall become your Values.
Understand and embrace your Values, for they become your Destiny."

These words spoken by *Mahatma Gandhi,* one of the world's greatest statesmen, preeminent leader of non-violent independence movements, founder and father of Modern India, gifted politician and philosopher, have always impressed me as the most exquisite and comprehensive explanation of the effect of thought in our life and living. Few people will dispute the fact that the quality and content of our daily thoughts have a direct bearing on our life and on the condition and other circumstances of our living. Your thoughts are dictating and influencing your every action during each waking moment and even when you are asleep. Each action you perform, every thing you perceive, every plan you develop and every decision you make has its origin in that poorly understood inner world of your thoughts. They are the key to your world and unless you are able the take control of them and direct them, they will surely destroy you, even as they paradoxically act to protect you.

From the dawn of civilization, the greatest thinkers and philosophers have wrestled with the problem of understanding and explaining the origin and influence of thought on human behavior. The ancient Chinese schools of thought including *Confucianism* and *Taoism,* that flourished 4000 years ago during the period known as the *Golden Age of Chinese Philosophy* offered many theories but no real answers. So too, during the period of enlightenment of the *Ancient Greco-Roman* era led by philosophers such as *Socrates, Plato* and *Aristotle*, fathers of modern philosophy, as well as during the subsequent *Indian-Persian Era*, dominated by the teachings of *Hinduism, Buddhism* and *Zarathustra*, man has searched for answers, offered many theories but with no conclusions. In fact, our state of knowledge today, despite thousands of years of search and study, has not significantly advanced, and we are still at the point of offering theories, not conclusions.

The power of thought is the master key in creating and maintaining the person who you are. Left uncontrolled, it is driven by a relentless desire to "protect" you at all cost, even when that cost is your self-destruction. Just consider the unfortunate outcome of the severely Obsessive Compulsive patient who is driven by his abnormal thoughts to commit repetitive actions that are useless, non-productive and destructive and which so enslave the victim that they become imprisoned in a world of their own making. Equally, consider the victims of drug and alcohol abuse, in which the over-riding thoughts of self-gratification drive them inexorably into the hell of addiction. Then there are the unfortunate victims of pathological thinking as in *Depression* and in *Schizophrenia* which, if not corrected, will lead to frightening conclusions. In all of these instances, the single dominant culprit is the victim's thought processes which have gone astray and resist correction or control.

To become master of your life, you must learn to control the nature and the content of your thoughts. By doing so you will be able to bring order, make choices and exercise options related to the actual and prevailing circumstances of your life. By controlling instinctive thoughts and replacing them with relevant options, you will in effect, bring order and reality to your living and avoid the destructive influence of negative thinking. By doing so, you will be able to choose your direction, exercise your options and plan and predict your future course based, not on blind impulse, but on considered action. It is important that we understand that the mind, if not controlled, will react automatically in the direction to which it is conditioned and imprinted. Negative thoughts, if not altered, will automatically influence everything you do, or feel, or say and your life will be dominated by this negativity which will then become the standard of behavior.

It is for this reason that Gandhi's advice is so definitive, as he carefully traces the sequence of events from the initiation of a single thought to the ultimate expression of one's final destiny. Indeed, I have no doubt that anyone of us with very little effort will have no difficulty in recalling examples of this happening in our own lives on a daily basis. This is why it is so very important that we take time and effort to teach our children the importance of critical review of thought processes and to avoid, at all cost, the tendency to respond and react impulsively because, "it sounds good", or "it makes sense".

Napoleon Hill, the great American author and one of the most successful inspirational and self-help pioneers summarized this most effectively in the following quotation:

"Life is a mirror of your consistent thoughts."

Man's greatness lies in his power of thought.
.........Blaise Pascal

The wise ones fashioned speech with their thought,
Sifting it as grain is sifted through a sieve.
.......Buddha

Some men use thought only as authority for their injustice,
And employ speech only to conceal their thoughts.
......Voltaire

I have always thought the actions of men,
Are the best interpreters of their thoughts.
.......John Locke

Thoughts are living things. A thought is as much solid as a piece of
stone. We may cease to be, but our thoughts can never die.
..... Sri Swami Sivananda

The greatest weapon against stress,
Is our ability to choose one thought over another.
......William James

Shutting off the thought process is not rejuvenating.
The mind is like a car battery, it recharges by running.
........Bill Watterson

Life with Courage

"Courage is the greatest of all the virtues.
Because if you haven't courage,
you may not have an opportunity to use any of the others."

*L*ike the great English writer, poet and essayist Samuel Johnson, I too believe Courage is the most universally respected and admired of all man's virtues. Contrary to popular opinion, Courage is not dealing with a situation with reckless abandon, nor meeting a challenge without regard to consequences. To me, courage is a much more complex and comprehensive set of behavioral characteristics arising from one's beliefs about life and how one chooses to live life. Aristotle, the ancient Greek philosopher, described it accurately as:

"Courage is the first of human qualities;
Because it is the quality that guarantees all the others."

The act of Courage is much more than the facing of a danger or taking on a challenge. It is a quality of spirit that enables you to act appropriately in the face of unexpected challenges. It is the strength of character that allows you to face apparent obstacles or dangers or the unknown with measured responses and a commitment to succeed. Equally, it can also be seen in situations when facing defeat knowingly in order to fulfill a greater cause. Perhaps the best example of this in American history is the famous Battle of the Alamo when a small garrison of less than 100 volunteers stood up to the Mighty Mexican Army of

Santa Ana for 13 days allowing the American army enough time to regroup and ultimately defeat the Mexicans.

Like most human characteristics, courage is not inherited and is not present at birth, but is developed and nurtured gradually by learning and by exposure to risk taking. Children who are not afforded the opportunity to meet and deal with challenges are necessarily lacking this ability and invariably find difficulty in responding to situations with the level of courage needed. To be managed successfully, it requires the use of all the elements of human behavior. Unlike the blind, impulsive response of a Rage Reaction which is nothing but an innate animal response, true courage draws on a complex mix of human characteristics including experience, maturity, intelligence, confidence and logic. To be successful the response must be balanced and directed, with a definitive, realistic goal.

Examples of Courage and Courageous behavior abound all around us but most of the time we do not recognize them. Some are easy to recognize such as when a police officer faces an armed assailant, his action is one of supreme courage, similarly when a soldier is sent in harm's way, he carries his courage each time, for they know they risk serious consequences. In other situations Courage is expressed in the form of commitment. When Muhammad Ali refused Army conscription because of his religious beliefs and as a result suffered the indignities of losing all his reputation, that too, was an act of courage, no different than when John McCain refused freedom from a North Vietnam prison in solidarity with the other prisoners who were not offered the same opportunity.

But there is another form of Courage that often goes unnoticed but one which serves a vital purpose in the life of a society. Some people have referred to this aspect as Moral Courage, a name that I consider quite appropriate. It's when the individual speaks out in situations where there are blatant transgressions. When the hotel maid accuses the powerful French politician of impropriety, or the office clerk reports the gross financial manipulations of the CEO, or the staff employee exposes the blatant lying of a sitting President or the clinic nurse speaks out on the mistreatment of long-stay patients in her institution; these are all examples of true courage. They serve to reinforce the principles of a good society and to ensure a decent quality of life to all its members.

There is no denying that courage is expressed in millions of diverse ways by so many of us without any concern of gain or reward. The only consideration is the intention to do the right thing at all cost. This above all, is the essential component for leading a life of fulfillment and satisfaction. As *Maya Angelou*, the celebrated Florida-based, African-American poet, noted:

> *"One isn't necessarily born with Courage, but one is born with potential. Without Courage, we cannot practice any other virtue with consistency. We can't be kind, true, merciful, generous, or honest".*

> *Courage is the first of human qualities*
> *because it is the quality which guarantees the others.*
> *……..Aristotle*

> *Courage is what it takes to stand up and speak,*
> *Courage is also what it takes to sit down and listen.*
> *……Sir Winston Churchill*

> *Often the test of courage is not to die but to live.*
> *……. Vittorio Alfieri*

> *Courage is simply the willingness to be afraid and act anyway.*
> *……. Robert Anthony*

> *It is a wise man who knows where courage ends and stupidity begins.*
> *…….Jerome Cady*

> *All our dreams can come true, if we have the courage to pursue them.*
> *…… Walt Disney*

> *From caring comes courage.*
> *……. Lao Tzu*

The courage to be, is the courage to accept oneself,
in spite of being unacceptable.
. . . . . . .Paul Tillich

Optimism is the foundation of Courage.
. . . . . . Nicholas Butler

Courage is the price that Life exacts for granting Peace
. . . . . . .Amelia Earhart

Courage is never to let your actions be influenced by your fears.
. . . . . . .Arnold Koesttler

It isn't life that matters! It is the Courage you bring to it.
. . . . . .Sir Hugh Walpole

Courage is the capacity to move ahead in spite of despair.
. . . . .Rollo May

Courage does not always roar like a lion;
Sometimes it is the quiet voice inside that is saying;
. "I will try again tomorrow."
. . . . .Mary Ann Radmachar

Courage is being scared to death; and saddling up anyway.
. . .John Wayne

He who does not have Courage enough to take risks,
will accomplish nothing in life.
. . . . . . .Muhammad Ali

A man of Courage is also full of faith. Courage is contagious.
When a brave man takes a stand, the spines of others are often stiffened.
...... *Billy Graham*

I've learned that Courage is not the absence of fear, but the triumph over it.
.... *Nelson Mandela*

Courage is not the absence of despair;
It is rather, the capacity to move ahead in spite of despair.
...... *Rollo May*

Life and Anger

"*The intoxication of anger, like that of the grape, shows us to others, but hides us from ourselves.*"

These words, written by *John Dryden*, the great English poet and literary critic of the sixteenth century, crystallize the true impact of anger upon the individual. Most Psychologists view anger as a primary emotion experienced by all humans at some time or another. To an extent, it forms an integral part of the "flight or fight" survival mechanism. In the right context, anger can be used to mobilize psychological resources for corrective action while at other times it becomes a destructive force to the individual's psyche. Uncontrolled Anger is a strong word describing a serious human emotion to which we are all subject to varying degrees. It is a feeling that is oriented toward some real or supposed grievance, associated with distrust and displeasure. It is usually accompanied with the loss of control and an inability to institute corrective actions to regain it. It can seriously affect personal and social well-being and seriously compromises quality of life.

Except in situations of "righteous indignation", Society universally frowns on anger and people who use it indiscriminately. So too do all the religions. Christianity considers it a Cardinal Sin and in Hinduism, anger is equated with sorrow as a form of "unrequited desire". The Quran attributes anger as an enemy of the Prophet and the Torah records "*he that is hasty of temper exalteth folly*". Buddhism rejects anger, including it as one of the "five hindrances". In all of them anger is reserved solely for the Gods.

I cannot think of anyone, including myself, who is not guilty of responding to threatened situations with inappropriate anger over and over again, only to find that rather than solve the conflict, we inevitably aggravate the situation. Anger is never productive, because we inevitably lose a lot more than we ever gain. My own personal experience confirms this. So many times I responded in anger to situations for which at the time I felt justified, only realizing subsequently that no resolution occurred and worse, the situation was further compromised.

As I have grown older I have gradually acquired the maturity to learn that in conflict situations patience is a far greater asset than anger, and that much more resolution is achieved by resisting the impulse to explode, than any other action. So often is it the case that when the truth is eventually exposed, to find that the reasons for the initial angry response turns out to be questionable, and the outburst was totally unjustified.

Nowadays, I am often guided by the advice of a good friend and relative, who constantly reminds me that in any conflict situation, *"You don't get angry, you get even"*. Whenever I can, I take every opportunity to pass this advice to all. For in the end you can do no better than to be guided by the words of the Bible, contained in Romans 12:19:

"Never avenge yourselves, but leave it to the wrath of God"

He who angers you conquers you.
.......Elizabeth Kenny

Anger dwells only in the bosom of fools.
.......Albert Einstein

Anger blows out the lamp of the mind.
.......Robert G. Ingersoll

Holding on to anger is like grasping a hot coal, with intent of throwing it at someone else. You are the one who gets burnt.
.....Buddha

Consider how much more you often suffer from your anger and grief,
than from those very things for which you are angry and grieved.
. . . . Marcus Antonius

Anger is one letter short of danger.
. . . . Author Unknown

For every minute you remain angry, you give up sixty
seconds of peace of mind.
. . . . .Ralph Waldo Emerson

How much more grievous are the consequences of anger
than the causes of it.
. . . . Marcus Aurelius

Life with Hypocrisy

"On December 11, 2009, one of the greatest golfers of all time announced he would take an indefinite leave from professional golf to focus on his marriage after he admitted infidility. His multiple infidelities were revealed with more than a dozen mistresses through many worldwide media sources."

This statement reported by CNBC exposed one of the greatest hyprocrites of modern times. He, who for years had projected by word, deed and action the image of a clean, committed and dedicated family man, was in fact leading a life that was a gross abomination to the sanctity and honor of his marriage. But his is not the only instance of this kind of behavior. Recently, more that thirty women have publicly accused a very popular comedian, a man who built his reputation on wholesome family life, of drugging and raping them. By any measure these are classic examples of Hypocrites.

The truth is that hypocrisy is probably the most common of human actions, far surpassing all other examples of human transgressions. The description of the hypocrite is one who pretends to have "good" intentions while having antagonistic intentions or convictions. It is pretending to be someone you really are not or pretending to be better than someone else. Hypocrisy in one form or another, takes place everyday and everywhere, in our schools, workplaces, government and our churches. It occurs so frequently around us that we have become quite immune to its presence and except for a blatant transgression like the golfer's or comedian's action, we generally accept it without much comment. In fact there is no denying that when it suits us, we as guilty of hypocrisy as anyone else.

Throughout the ages, hypocrisy has always been, in one form or another, the foundation upon which nations have justified their actions in the conquering and domination of their citizens, and even of other nations. Leaders, by and large, have been able to reach and survive at the top by the successful hypocritical manipulation of their subordinates, and politicians, to a very large extent, have generally survived and prospered by their effective use of hypocrisy.

No institution has been more effective and more successful in the use of hypocrisy than the Religions of the world. History abounds with examples of hypocrisy among all the great religions whose leaders have had no hesitation to use it to further their own causes. Consider the "Inquisitions" conducted by the Roman Catholic Church during the Middle Ages, when thousands were tortured and burnt at the stakes in the name of stamping out "heretics". No better, were the Crusaders who, in the name of Christianity and the saving of Jerusalem, carried out a ruthless program of rape and destruction of the Moslem countries they conquered.

The Holy Bible contains more references to hypocrisy than almost any other topic. The most famous reference of these is recorded in *Matthew 23:24,* when Jesus admonished the clerics in the Synagogue thus:

> *"Woe unto you, Scribes and Pharisees, hypocrites!, for ye pay tithe of mint and anise and cumin, and have omitted the weightier matters of the law, judgment, mercy, and faith: these ought ye to have done, and not to leave the other undone. Ye blind guides, which strain at a gnat, and swallow a camel."*

In recent years it appears that hypocrisy has gained even greater popularity, to the point where it has become part of modern day life. It is a crying shame when the President of a great nation initiates a war in the name of fighting terrorism by concocting false information. Or a Priest stands on the alter delivering a sermon on the sanctity of the family, while actively involved in the abuse of young parishioners. Or the senior executives of a bank that required massive infusion of public funds to survive, accepting large bonuses while thousands of home owners were being foreclosed upon as a result of the executives' incompetence and immoral actions. By any standards their actions cry out to heaven for vengeance!

Hannah Arendt, the celebrated German-Jewish philosopher who died in 1973, openly criticized the actions of hypocrites in the following terms in her publication, *On Revolution:*

> *"The hypocrite's crime is that he bears false witness against himself. What makes it so plausible to assume that hypocrisy is the vice of vices is that integrity can indeed exist under the cover of all other vices except this one. Only crime and the criminal, it is true, confront us with the perplexity of evil; but only the hypocrite is really rotten to the core".*

In the end, the responsibility of each one of us is to have the courage to confront and to expose and reject any form of hypocrisy we encounter with as much enthusiasm as we can muster. If enough of us succeed, I have no doubt that in the end our voices will be heard and corrective action will follow. The golfer's life for example, has undergone a substantial transformation since his admission. He has lost his family, his game has faltered very badly and his reputation has been permanently tarnished. He has indeed paid a significant price for his transgressions.

> *Most of us are aware of and pretend to detest the barefaced instances of that hypocrisy by which men deceive others, but few of us are upon our guard or see that more fatal hypocrisy by which we deceive and over-reach our own hearts.*
> *......Laurence Sterne,*

> *Every man alone is sincere. At the entrance of a second person, hypocrisy begins. We parry and fend the approach of our fellow-man by compliments, by gossip, by amusements, by affairs. We cover up our thought from him under a hundred folds.*
> *.......Ralph Waldo Emerson, from "Friendship Essays"*

Hypocrisy is oftenest clothed in the garb of religion
........*Hosea Ballou.*

The only vice that cannot be forgiven is Hypocrisy.
The repentance of an hypocrite is itself hypocrisy.
.........*William Hazlitt*

The true Hypocrite is the one who ceases to perceive his deception, the
one who lies with sincerity.
.........*André Gide*

A Hypocrite is the kind of politician who would cut down a redwood
tree, then mount the stump and make a speech for conservation.
.......*Adlai E. Stevenson*

SECTION 4

Life with People

We are never meant to live in isolation, but to share our space and our feelings with others.

From its very inception this world was formulated to accommodate different people living together in a common good.

Our lives can be affected, directly or indirectly, by others, or others can be affected by us. It remains to us to accept some and reject the others.

Along the way, people may also impact us by their actions in such a way as to leave an indelible impression for good or bad.

These are lessons we must learn as we travel along The Road of Life.

Life with Molly
A short story of Faith, Fate and Coincidence

"A bizarre accident occurred on the highway early this morning. It claimed the lives of three people, one of whom is yet to be identified. A large Hummer crossed the median at high speed and ploughed into the smaller Kia vehicle, killing all the occupants. The driver of the Hummer, who was returning from an all night "stag party" celebrating his upcoming wedding due to be held today, was unharmed. His breathalyzer test was very strongly positive."

Violet sat up when she heard those words spoken by the radio announcer who was reporting a newsflash that had just been received. Something in her told her that this was not good and for some strange reason she thought of Molly. She listened carefully, but no more information was forthcoming. All day she listened to the radio, but not another word was said. It felt as if a blackout was in effect. She just could not stop worrying.

That night as she sat down to have dinner with her husband, the phone rang. It was Virginia enquiring about her mother who had not arrived home yet, and none of her friends or family knew anything. Violet, shuddering with anticipation, blurted out *"Have you called the police? Have you checked with the hospital?"* For some strange reason, ever since hearing the announcement she could not shift the thought that Molly was involved. She was not surprised when Virginia called back early next morning confirming that Molly was indeed involved in the accident and had died before any help could arrive. She also added that the only way she could have identified her mother was by the silver cross she was wearing. This was the cross that was given to Molly last Xmas by Violet's father with love and appreciation, for her dedicated care to his wife, who suffered from Advanced Alzheimer's.

For more than five years Molly had been the live-in caregiver who would come to the house early Monday morning and leave early Saturday morning. A gentle, caring person in her late 50's, she was a devotedly religious person who loved people and was dedicated to her role of caring for the weak and helpless. She endeared herself so deeply to the family that she became part of the family and was loved by all, as indeed, she loved them. Violet was particularly close to her, and they shared a bond as close as sisters. They would spend many hours sharing and praying together, as they jointly took care of the needs of the old people. -They were sisters in spirit.

As she recalled the events of the hours before Molly's death, Violet became increasingly overwhelmed with a sense of awe at the power of Fate in life, and wondered whether life is truly predestined and beyond our control. The night before, after dinner was completed and the old people settled, Molly informed Violet that she planned to leave much earlier than usual as she was getting a lift with some friends. She planned to leave at 6:00am. Violet could not understand why she felt compelled to caution her but recalled saying: *"Are you sure that is a good idea. Why do you want to leave that early?"*

The next morning Molly got up at the crack of dawn and was ready to leave as early as 5:00am. She called Violet who would normally come over to relieve her. However Violet was unable to get over because of a flare up of her ankle sprain and asked her to wait a little longer to allow the "Advil" she took to start working. Molly called back to inform her that her friends were insisting on leaving early and as a result she was committed to leave on time. Violet recalled her last words to Molly were, *"Go with God, may he take care of you on your journey home!"*

Molly left the home at 5:45am and walked to the corner to wait for her friends. When she got there, she realized that she had left her cross at home and quickly returned to retrieve it. On arriving home, she encountered the old man who was in the kitchen drinking a cup of coffee that Molly had prepared and left for him. After she explained why she had returned, he stood up, held her hand firmly and said with a deliberate, serious tone;

"Molly please stay back for a while. In our culture it is a bad omen to begin a journey and to return before it is completed. I want you to stay!"

She chuckled and replied as she snapped the cross around her neck, *"Grandpa I am protected with this cross. Nothing could happen to me!"* She then quickly exited to meet her friends.

The police reported that the Kia was traveling south at normal speed in light traffic when the Hummer which was traveling north at very high speed suddenly swerved to the left, missed a light pole and crashed directly into the car. The Kia was smashed beyond recognition and all the occupants killed instantly. The cross was found in Molly's right hand as she apparently grasped it in her final moments.

Like Violet, we are all left to wonder the meanings of Fate and Faith. Many will be content to assign these events as merely examples of coincidence which occur every day to every body. Others, like my friend Lawrence, will often respond in these situations with a confident and reassuring, *"No Big Thing, it happens everyday!"* I prefer to think of these events as occurring beyond our control and as such, beyond our human comprehension. But I share Violet's view that in some unexplained way, this was the hand of God working. Perhaps this was a way of warning us of impending disaster. We will never know!

In this context I am reminded of a statement made by an unknown contributor on the "This I Believe" Series on National Public Radio which stated:

"We, as humans can do nothing but live in the present.
We cannot see what is to come in the future.
We can only guess and attempt to make the right choices."

--*Unfortunately, for whatever reason, Molly made the wrong choice!*

Life in the Time of Joan Baez

*I*n 1959, as a recent Medical Graduate newly returned to my home in Trinidad, my attention was drawn to a young American woman named Joan Baez, who had briefly visited the island. She was described as a folk singer with a beautiful voice. Indeed when I heard her rendition of *"We are crossing the Jordan River"* at the Newport Folk Festival, I immediately recognized the beauty and clarity of her voice and have continued to enjoy her works since then. I have followed her career over the last 50 years and have made every effort to acquire her complete works. Despite the passage of time, she continues to amaze me with her renditions and remains my favorite artist.

Yet, however successful her singing career has become, it is dwarfed by her life-long and determined drive to make this world better by her continued activism in the areas of nonviolence, civil and human rights. She is a wonderful example of a true humanitarian. Quite unlike the great majority of successful artists who choose to advertise their success with notoriety, drug and alcohol abuse and sexual adventures. One only has to compare the life styles and histories of the current popular entertainers to that of Joan Baez to appreciate her true contribution to society, as compared to the generally negative contributions of the others.

Her early years were spent deeply involved in supporting the civil rights movement led by Martin Luther King Jr. Her rendition of *"We shall overcome"* at the 1963 *March on Washington* remains a classic, as it moved the hundreds of thousands of protesters to tumultuous applause. She participated in many of these marches, entertaining the crowds with her songs and her singing.

She was also very prominent in the anti-Vietnam war protests and rallies. She organized a free concert at the Washington Monument in Washington, DC, attended by a crowd of over 30,000, to the loud objections of the establishment. She was also very involved in protesting local and international human rights violations.

In 1970 she helped in establishing the US branch of *Amnesty International* and worked to expose violations in the US as well as places as diverse as Vietnam, Cambodia, Chile, Brazil and Argentina. She established her own human rights group, *Humanitas International*, to target oppression anywhere it occurred. Her struggles have not slowed with age, presently she remains active in such diverse causes as Gay rights, Environmental abuses, Death penalty and the Iraq war and shows no sign of slowing down. She has received many acknowledgements and honors along the way including honorary *Doctor of Humane Letters* from Antioch and Rutgers Universities for her "political activism and her music".

Perhaps you will now understand why I have chosen to call the last 50 years "The Time of Joan Baez" and to appreciate how this one committed woman, blessed with the gift of a beautiful voice, could do so much to help her world and its people.

Can you say the same for the great majority of entertainers and other personalities that constantly inhabit the news magazines and the television screens?

Some Quotations from the mind of Joan Baez:

-To love means you also trust.

-You don't get to choose how you're going to die...or When.

-You can only decide if you're going to live...and How.
Action is the antidote to despair.

-I do not believe in war.
I do not believe in the weapons of war

-I've been obsessed with stopping people from blowing each other's brains out since I was ten.

-You may not know it, but at the far end of despair, there is a white clearing where one is almost happy.

-That's all nonviolence is - organized love

My concern has always been for the people, who are victimized, unable to speak for themselves and who need outside help As long as one keeps searching, the answers come.

Life with Mary
A Study of Simple Faith and Love

I have never seen her, but I believe I know her. If she were to walk past me now, I will not recognize her, yet I am sure I know her. If she were to stop me and speak to me, I know that her voice will not be familiar, yet I know, I know her. Her name is Mary, that's all I know, yet she has been as familiar to me as my next door neighbor. All I know about Mary, I know from my wife, Gloria, yet as far as I am concerned, it is as if I have known her all my life.

Gloria knows her as the kind, cheerful cleaning lady who has been working at the local park for the past 6 years. Always with a large beaming smile, she greeted every one of the regulars with a hug so big and so reassuring that you instinctively sensed her sincerity. *"I missed you Glo",* she would say to Gloria whenever a day is missed from the usual morning routine. *"The ducks are doing fine"* she would add, *"but they miss you too".*

Mary first came to my attention almost four years ago when Gloria would come home from her regular morning visit to the park and speak glowingly of this truly "Christian lady" whose faith in God was so complete and powerful. Despite having to deal with the terminal illness of her only son who at the time was readmitted to hospital for the last time, she still found the peace of mind to praise God and trust in his ultimate plans for her son. When any of the regulars in the park will enquire about the boy, she would invariably reply with a smile grounded in her faith in her God, and quietly say:

"He is in the hands of Jesus, and by His stripes he is healed"

And when he subsequently succumbed to the ravages of his illness, Mary took a few days off to mourn and then returned to the park to continue her work. Even with a heart laden with grief, she continued to smile and greet the regulars with words of support and encouragement and a heartfelt prayer to *"Praise Jesus, Thank you Jesus for everything"*. When someone will offer her sympathy at her recent loss, she would reply with profound pride and conviction, *"Thank you Jesus, he is now a soldier in Jesus' army"*

Like so many others, Mary's early life was spent in the pursuit of personal pleasure without any regard to personal pride or dignity. Mixing with the wrong people, she was oblivious to the demands of decency and self respect. She was lost, and did not care about consequences. She was clearly oblivious, or at least unconcerned about her downward path into personal damnation. She neglected every one who meant anything to her and was not bothered with her family responsibility and the care of her only son. That meant nothing to her.

She recalls her moment of truth taking place on a fateful day when she found herself among people who worshiped Satan and being invited to become one. This was enough to create such an alarming response that she ran out in shear terror and immediately sought out a Christian church. The events which then occurred are indelibly printed in her brain and she does not miss any opportunity to relate them to anyone who will listen. She refers to the occurrence as, *"her conversion"*, when in desperation she opened a bible and in spite of the fact that she could not read, she swears that she was able to read and understand the written words. *Christ was alive and his message was one of love and forgiveness to all sinners.*

From then on, like Mary Magdalene of old after her own conversion, she became a devoted follower of Jesus Christ. Her message is simple. She loves everyone as brothers and sisters, bears no malice towards anyone and prays for all people. *She is now a true soldier for Jesus.* Her life is now spent in living and spreading the message. Her faith is strong and her belief in God's love and goodness is unshakable. Her life is spent in helping wherever she can, sharing and supporting whenever the need arises and taking care of those in need in whatever way possible. This extends to all living creatures including the wild birds in the park.

In her own very simple way, Mary has found the true way of life that all good Christians aspire and hope for. She has no material riches to show and does not ever wear designer clothes. In fact whatever clothes she accumulates, she is likely to pass on to one of her needy church brothers or sisters. But unlike the "Madonnas" and the "Kimyes" of the world, she is not lost anymore. She does not have to spend all her days accumulating wealth and recognition, while searching for the next pleasure or the next adoring fan. She knows that she is truly loved by the one person who matters.

Rather, she spends her days in the way he has taught us to do, by loving her neighbors as herself, forgiving others who trespass against her and giving glory to her God.

. . . . .Is it any surprise that Mary is sought after by so many of the regulars in the park when they feel the need to pray?

For you were called to freedom, brothers. Only do not use your freedom as an opportunity for the flesh, but through love serve one another.
. . . .Galatians 5:13

We are all God's children so it is important to share His gifts.
Do not worry about why problems exist in the world
just respond to people's needs
. . . .Blessed Teresa of Kolkata

"It is one of the most beautiful compensations of life; that no man can sincerely try to help another without helping himself."
. . . . .Ralph Waldo Emerson

Instead of asking: "If I stop to help this man, what will happen to me?" Be like the Good Samaritan and ask: "If I do not stop to help this man, what will happen to him?"
. . . . .Martin Luther King, Jr.

"El Sistema"
Lessons from the Barrios of Venezuela

"Ask him about it, and he'll tell you he owes it all to a remarkable program in his native Venezuela, a social program that has used music to change his own life and the lives of millions of children there. Venezuelans call it "El Sistema," "The System," and Dudamel wants to bring it to the U.S., where he believes it can work wonders."

These words were spoken by a CBS reporter, the late *Bob Simon*, as he introduced the great Venezuelan conductor, *Gustavo Dudamel*, the 29 year old, internationally acclaimed conductor of the Los Angeles Philharmonic Orchestra, on a recent *"60 Minutes"* television program. He then went on to describe Dudamel's accomplishments since coming to the United States. He was by far the youngest maestro and the most exciting conductor of any major orchestra in the world.

Amazing as this achievement was, the real story, which Simon went into great detail to elaborate, revolved around the work of a retired Venezuelan economist, social reformer and amateur musician, *Dr. Jose' Antonio Abreu*, who founded "El Sistema" *(The System)* as a vehicle to deal with the large and growing problem of poverty, crime and illiteracy in the *barrios of Caracas*, the capital city of Venezuela.

His approach was based on the conviction that exposure to the discipline and spiritual richness provided by classical music can achieve personal and social change among the most disenfranchised and hopeless sections of society. Starting in 1975 with this idea that children would learn the discipline needed to succeed by exposure to classical music, he enlisted the help of a few fellow

154

musicians. Some donated instruments and with 11 students he began his first "cell". This concept quickly exploded as parents and students realized the great satisfaction and rewards derived from their efforts. It rapidly grew to include thousands of children from ages as early as 2 years, scattered in the worst areas of the society spread across Venezuela. It now involves over 270,000 participants, organized in at least 60 children orchestras, 200 youth orchestras, 30 professional orchestras and many choirs, producing world class music.

In addition there are various workshops teaching construction and repair of instruments, and a variety of specialized clinics providing remedial and therapy programs for impaired children. The great majority of these facilities are provided free of charge to all participants.

Since its inception, El Sistema has produced over 800,000 graduates. The orchestras have performed all over the world with universal acclaim and have produced musicians who now play in most of the world's greatest orchestras. The most prominent and most respected product is *Dudamel*, who presently leads the Los Angeles Orchestra. Like every disciple of the "System", Dudamel is driven to spread the concept all over the world and in fact, as Simon suggested:

> "Dudamel was so sought after; he could have conducted almost anywhere. He chose Los Angeles in part because he thought it was a good place to transplant the system to the U.S".

Since arriving in Los Angeles, Dudamel has donated a great deal of time to developing the Youth Orchestra of Los Angeles (YOLA), with the explicit intention of following the pattern set in Venezuela to *"transform the lives of thousands of L.A. youth through music",* and then by example, to spread the message nationwide. By all accounts, this venture has already begun to produce positive results, and in addition to Los Angeles, cells have been started in Baltimore and Chicago.

Even as we celebrate the genius of Dr. Abreau's efforts and must recognize the unqualified success of his system in the rehabilitation and preservation of thousands of young lives in the *barrios* of Venezuela, let us not forget that there are lessons to be learnt that can be applied to our own society. With the increasing incidence of violence and indiscriminate drug use in our schools, there is urgent need to address the deteriorating situation. In this regard, I am convinced that our educational system, by its increasingly liberal and less structured approach has lost its way. This is compounded by the lack of parental influence and concern and the children's increasing exposure to the negative effects of the modern TV/Video Games/Texting capabilities which serve to cheat them of the all-important opportunity of developing self-image. We are producing a generation of uncontrolled, self-serving people who have been left alone and have never been given the opportunity to really know who they are.

The strength of "El Sistema" is that it succeeds in attracting young minds and by dint of commitment and discipline, producing a mature, confident individual capable of carrying out complex, meaningful and rewarding activity. Whether this translates to a career in music or otherwise, the end result is the production of a motivated individual with a positive attitude to life and to society. Gretchen Nielsen, the YOLA philharmonic's education director, very accurately summarized these sentiments thus:

> *"I think we're really striving to change the landscape of Los Angeles. We want to see these kids graduate. We want to see them just connect to the world in ways that they might not have normally otherwise ....And we want to see it across this city."*

This indeed is the real lesson to be learnt from the *Barrios of Venezuela,* and from the genius of a retired Venezuelan economist with a love for music who built "El Sistema" with *"religious zeal, based on his unorthodox belief that what poor Venezuelan kids needed was classical music" (Bob Simon).*

Perhaps the world's politicians, teachers and parents will one day wake up to their responsibilities, and take back control from the streets, drug dealers, television, video games, texting and facebook, and help the children reach their full potential.

The Barrios have taught us that this is indeed possible!

Reference Links:

http://www.cbsnews.com/stories/2008/04/11/60minutes/
main4009335_page4.shtml?tag=contentMain;contentBody
http://www.cbsnews.com/stories/2010/05/14/60minutes/
main6483731.shtml?tag=contentMain;cbsCarousel

A Tale of Two Disabilities
(Nick Vujicic / Tony Melendez)

"He could easily have played the victim in his life. Instead he chose to overcome his disabilities and be an inspiration to others because of his perseverance to live a normal life. By doing so, he seems to be living a blessed life in many ways. I know I felt blessed that I was able to see this man perform live. It was indeed an uplifting experience."

These words were written by a reporter whose name I do not recall, but who spoke for all of us who had experienced those wonderful feelings that overwhelmed us all after listening to a recital from the great inspirational singer, *Tony Melendez*. The recital was performed in Los Angeles, California in September, 1987 in honor of the late Pope John Paul II. It so moved the Pontiff that he rose from his chair and walked across to embrace him. This feat was even more impressive when one considered that Melendez was born without arms and played the guitar with his feet.

José Antonio Meléndez Rodríguez was born in Nicaragua in 1962. He was a thalidomide baby, born without arms, whose early life was one of intense loneliness. He was continuously subjected to ridiculing and bullying by his peers in school. They did not hesitate to remind him of his physical handicap (*'No tiene brazos'*). Being profoundly disabled caused him to feel intensely depressed and he would often express these feelings in such statements as "My heart hurts, it hurts me a lot" (*'Dolía el corazon. Me dolía mucho'*). His only escape was the guitar which he taught himself to play, using his feet and toes. His life changed positively when he saw the video of an Australian motivational speaker, almost 20 years younger than he was. It became a source of great inspiration to him and an answer for how he will spend the rest of his future life.

Nicholas James Vujicic was born in 1982 in Melbourne, Australia, the son of Croatian immigrants with a rare condition, *Tetramelia Disorder*, characterized by almost complete absence of his upper and lower limbs. After an early life filled with difficulty, including serious suicidal consideration when he was about 8 years old, He was allowed to enter mainstream school and with the help and encouragement from his teachers and together with use of gadgets and special devices to accommodate his disability, he was able to complete school and began a very successful career as a motivational Christian speaker. His motto is simple and to the point:

"Life without limbs,
No arms, No legs, No Worries"

Surprisingly, even without functioning arms or legs, his life is still much like that of any normal person. He cooks his food, does computer work, answers his phone, listens to music, plays golf, and goes into the swimming pool. He has remained very active visiting at least 26 countries to deliver his message with great success. He credits this turnaround to a newspaper article he read when he was about 13 years old, about a disabled man who had managed to achieve great things and help many people. As a result, he resolved to dedicate his life to follow this new ministry. He firmly believes that God has given him the strength to overcome what others might call insurmountable hurdles, and has placed in him a passion to share the hopes and genuine love he feels for everyone.

Isn't it strange, that these two men with severely profound disabilities, although born 6000 miles apart, under different circumstances and cultures, should eventually find a common way of overcoming their handicap and a genuine reason for living and helping others. Even more so, they were both able to rise from the depth of their despair and hopelessness as a result of a message from others in similar circumstances. They both credit their commitment to the service for God by the strong feeling that God was using them and their testimony to touch thousands of hearts around the world.

But we should not be surprised that God does indeed act in mysterious ways for the good of his people. Throughout our lives we all encounter, or hear of instances of in which people have behaved in extraordinary ways for the benefit of others. As Vujicic correctly noted on his website:

> *"Be encouraged today as you read this promise from the Lord found in Jeremiah 29:11 of the Bible, "For I know the plans I have for you, declares the Lord, plans to prosper you and not to harm you, plans to give you hope and a future."*

Disability is a matter of perception. If you can do just one thing well,
-You're needed by someone.
.......Martina Navratilova

The only disability in life is a bad attitude.
......Scott Hamilton

It is a waste of time to be angry about my disability. One has to get on with life and I haven't done badly. People won't have time for you if you are always angry or complaining.
...... Stephen Hawking

Disability is not a brave struggle or courage in the face of adversity. Disability is an art. It's an ingenious way to live.
......Neil Marcus

I discovered early that the hardest thing to overcome is not a physical disability, but the mental condition which it induces.
.....Alexander de Seversky

There is a plan and a purpose, a value to every life, no matter what its location, age, gender or disability.
....Sharron Angle

Willy, the Vagrant
A short story of honor and commitment

*T*he radio announcer on WUSF, 89.7, was solemn as he spoke:

> *"This is a breaking news item. A man is standing on a ledge of the Skyway Bridge on the south bound span preparing to jump into the deep blue waters of Tampa Bay more than 150 ft below. There are at least two Highway patrol troopers and a number of on-lookers on the scene. We will keep you informed as news come in."*

This was no surprise to me, or for that matter anyone who has lived in Tampa, Florida. Since its official opening in 1987, this beautiful, majestic piece of engineering spanning more than four miles across the bay, suspended by massive steel cables, has gained the unenviable reputation as the *Suicide Bridge of America*. Since its formal opening there have been more than two hundred successful attempts and at least fifty more individuals who lived to tell their story. This does not include the hundreds of others, male and female, who were persuaded to change their minds. The situation was taken so seriously by the authorities that in 1999 the State of Florida actually setup an action hotline with at least six stations along the bridge and a call center manned by specially trained personnel. They even went further and established a 24-hour patrol, which has operated continuously since then. Despite all these precautions, it is generally accepted that the site's popularity and the total number of jumpers have remained unchanged or may have increased.

Interestingly, it appears that all the potential jumpers who took time to call into the center ultimately survived, leaving people to speculate that these callers were not very serious about their intentions, but had adopted this action as a desperate call for help. It seems that those who were serious were always successful.

I was on my way to Ybor City to meet with my friend and colleague Robert, for our regular weekly beer, sandwich and cigar meeting. We have been meeting every single Wednesday for the past three years, hot, cold, dry or wet. We would try to get to the famous TBBC Restaurant on East 8th Street at 1pm, order a glass of Old Elephant Foot IPA, a Corned Beef Reuben for Robert and their famous Beer Battered Buffalo Chicken for myself and then finish off the afternoon with a Churchill Maduro select each.

Robert was the CPA for a group of physicians practicing in Lakeland, a small city about forty miles from Tampa. We met as undergraduate students at the University of Tampa and struck up a lasting friendship. We both enjoyed Basket Ball and would hit the courts as often as we could. We became even closer friends during the decade 1992-2002 when we traveled to Orlando to attend every Magic game, to see our common idol, Shaquille O'Neil, in action. After majoring in Psychology at U of T, I went on to complete a Law Degree at Stetson University and after a 2-year stint in the Army, was accepted by a local Law firm where I am presently practicing.

The announcer at WUSF broke in again to report that from the information received the man on the Skyway Bridge appeared to be a vagrant and kept referring to a Dr. Mike from the VA hospital, suggesting he might be a veteran in trouble. This immediately piqued my interest. For ever since my time in the army where as a young attorney with a psychology background I spent my time less fighting on the front lines and more on dealing with the psychological fallout on those young men and women who had gone to the front lines. Since then I have become more and more involved, and have devoted much of my spare time, energy and knowledge in helping my brothers and sisters. This was particularly so in respect of those suffering with that scourge of modern warfare commonly called Post Traumatic Stress Disorder (PTSD).

Without a second thought I knew what I must do. I was traveling on Kennedy drive and immediately changed direction towards 275 South heading to the Skyway. I called Robert on my Bluetooth and explained what I planned to do, he understood and he agreed. Our regular meeting was off. Once I got on the 275, I headed south over the Courtney Campbell Bridge and shortly after, the breathtaking view of the Skyway rising into the cloudless sky came into view. As I drove along toward the bridge I could see in the distance, a large commotion. There were at least two ambulances, an assortment of law enforcement vehicles and more than twenty cars, trucks and motorcycles with at least one hundred people milling around. At about one hundred yards away from the center of activities it was obvious that I could go no further, so I pulled off onto the shoulder, got out of the car and started to walk forward. As I got closer to the site, I could sense the excitement in the gathered crowd of onlookers. It was clearly a very serious situation.

There were several troopers standing close to the barrier and at least one of them who appeared to be a negotiator talking to the young man. He was a tall, thin athletic looking man in his mid-thirties with long, scruffy blond hair tied in a pony tail and an ungroomed beard clearly in need of a thorough shampoo and wash. His clothes were well fitting but obviously heavily used and in need of replacement or at least washing. He stood proud on the ledge of the bridge like a captain surveying the scene. His eyes were wide open, showing a clear set of blue corneas and despite all the commotion around him they appeared to be focused on the far horizon, completely oblivious of his immediate environment. He was a man on a mission.

When I got closer, I realized this young man was no stranger to me. I recognized him as William Brady whom I first met four or five years ago on the streets of Tampa while I worked as a volunteer with Volunteers of America of Florida. I got to know him quite well over a period of more than a year before he left the area to go to South Florida. He was Brother Willy to me and we spent many hours together as he suffered repeated episodes of traumatic recollections, his fears, his anxieties and above all, his social rejections.

Willy was born to a close-knit family in Kansas. His father is a retired Engineer and his mother was a teacher. He was a very active student who excelled in sports, especially long distance running, and was a straight-A student who was a biology whiz. He obtained a full scholarship to attend college where he studied Biology, obtaining his bachelor's degree cum laude. Upon completion he elected to follow his mother's vocation and take up teaching. Subsequently he applied and was accepted to teach Biology and Genetics in a high school in Ft. Lauderdale, Florida. He quickly became a sensation; not only with regard to his competence, but in the way he was able to motivate his students to achieve more. He very quickly took over all the AP Biology classes and they became much sought after. He also became involved in athletic activities especially in respect of marathon and cross-country running and very soon developed quite a successful program. Willy was a happy man, doing what he enjoyed, and gained the respect of his peers and his students for his efforts. He was even beginning to entertain the possibility of going further in education, applying for post-graduate studies and even proceeding into a college academic career.

Everything changed dramatically on March 19, 2003, when President George W. Bush gave the order to invade Iraq. Willy, having spent all of his high school and university years as an active member of the ROTC felt it was his duty to obey the order of his commander-in-chief. He promptly enlisted and very shortly after, found himself undergoing training in an Army Base in Tampa. By June he was on his way to Iraq as an Infantry man, by way of a forward base in Kuwait. His unit received orders to move out in early July, 2003 and on July 17, 2003, on his mother's birthday, he boarded a Humvee and proceeded in a convoy northward to Baghdad. They had traveled several days in Iraq without encountering any kind of resistance. They were relaxed and generally felt that it was all over, that the "shock and awe" plan had really worked and that their tour will be a "piece of cake". Then it happened, their Humvee drove over an IED and blew up! The driver and four of the soldiers died on the spot and every one of the others were seriously injured. Willy suffered a severe concussion and remained in coma for 72 hours before slowly regaining consciousness. He was repatriated to USA and remained in the Miami VA hospital for nearly two months before being subsequently discharged in November, 2003. He was declared fully recovered from his physical injuries but unfortunately continued to suffer from a severe Post Traumatic Stress Disorder.

His problems were just beginning. He had lost all his people skills and could not tolerate any kind of stress without developing recurrent acute anxiety symptoms. He tried to resume his teaching career, but quickly realized that his memory gaps and lack of patience made it impossible to continue. In fact he was incapable of holding even the simplest service jobs without sooner or later getting in trouble. He gradually drifted down the social scale and as expected, all his friends and associates drifted away. He eventually ended up doing whatever he could, even panhandling or selling newspapers at street corners to try to survive. In the last few years he became a confirmed vagrant living as best as he can. He had officially joined the sixty to seventy thousand veterans who were homeless on the streets of America on any given night, a number greater than the number of service personnel who died during all the wars since World War 11.

He moved from city to city, lived in alley ways or in empty boxes or electrical rooms and foraged at the back of groceries or restaurants for leftovers. Sometimes kind people will try to extend a helpful hand, but most of the time people generally avoided him and some will go out of their way to remove their children from his vicinity. I presume this is the reason why he only stayed in any place a short while before moving on. He was never able develop any lasting relationships or even casual friends. Even the local police, some of whom were themselves discharged veterans, showed little tolerance and often tended to harass them and encourage them to move on, to appease the upset citizens and angry parents. For someone like him, who cared so much for the welfare of children, this was the unkindest cut of all. Not only was he unable to do what he loved best, but he was being actively treated like an outcast in his own community.

The VA was not very helpful but not for want of trying. I suspect the main reason is the serious overload on the limited resources available. Dr. Mike Jacobs, his present psychologist, had been trying, as best he can, to help him, but unfortunately, the heavy workload and limited time available rendered his efforts impotent. It would seem that congress has no hesitation in authorizing billions of dollars for more airplanes and equipment that were essentially unnecessary or in some cases obsolete, but at the same time determined to hold down or even cut back on essential commitments to the overall care of these people whose only sin is that they served and sacrificed for their country.

Added to this, we must not forget that Society's attitude to its homeless veteran population is correlated to the actual conflict that produced these veterans. The veterans of World War II, a popular war that involved the entire population, were far better assimilated and cared for than those of the very unpopular and to some experts, unjustified Vietnam and Iraq/Afghanistan conflicts. Many may dispute this assumption but, in my own mind, I am convinced that these very unpopular wars have not, and will never, be accepted as a glorious chapter in the great American story. In short Willy and all his affected brothers and sisters are doomed to a life of despair.

The majority of the older homeless veterans I encountered saw active duty in Vietnam, but unfortunately their ranks are rapidly being filled by new "recruits" from the Iraq and Afghanistan conflicts. Even more tragically, these include both male and female soldiers with much more serious disabilities and even more serious management problems, often including children. Compounding this is the tragic consequences of the very large population of very seriously injured and maimed veterans who normally would have died from their wounds but who have survived as a result of the miraculous advances in medicine. Despite the yeoman services of such wonderful organizations as Volunteers of America, Wounded Warriors of America, Habitat for Humanity, Disabled Veterans Association and many more, the final picture is mind boggling. As a society, we are much more inclined to sweep this problem under the carpet and hope that its goes away, or leave it to others, as we continue to enjoy all the good things that America provides. If we are truly honest most of us will admit that we would rather spend time chasing the latest exploits of Gaga or Madonna, Kanye and Kim, Wade and LeBron rather than be bothered by Willy, the Vagrant.

-What a crying shame!

I finally reached close enough to make eye contact with Willy, and as I yelled at the top of my voice: *"Hold on Brother Willy, I want to talk with you"*, I am sure he moved his lip as if to say goodbye, as he dived headlong in obscurity.

I paused for a while then dropped on my knees, lamenting the tragic loss of yet another good young man with such great human potential. I could only think of the words my friend Robert, speaking for all of us sometime ago, when we discussed this topic at one of our lunch meetings. With a deep sigh of resignation said:

> "Isn't it ironic that George Bush, and Dick Cheney and Donald Rumsfeld and Paul Wolfowitz continue with their lives, living happily and doing very well if you please, while these young men and women, and so many others like them with so much to offer, are consigned to the rubbish heap of society with no chance of return".

Life's Optimist
Life with Helen Adam Keller

"The essence of Optimism is that it takes no account of the present. But it is a source of inspiration, of vitality and hope to some where others have resigned. It enables a man to hold his head high, to claim the future for himself, and not to abandon it to his enemy."

This statement recorded by *Dietrich Bonhoeffer*, the German Lutheran theologian and resistance leader encapsulates in a few words the true meaning of being an optimist.

Optimism in fact does not have a simple definition as it refers to the expectation that good things rather than bad things will happen. It is a concept where one looks upon the world as a positive place. Optimists generally believe that people are inherently good and that over time things will always work out favorably in the end. It is classically characterized in the example of the *glass that has been filled half way*. While the pessimist will lament that it is half empty, the optimist will rejoice that it was at least half full. Even in situations in which the outcome was less than expected, the optimist understands that it could not have been avoided, projects it as a flaw or mishap in his life, and quickly moves on.

Throughout the ages, in every aspect of life, optimism in one form or other has always been a fundamental component in successful outcomes. History is replete with examples of leaders whose successes have been achieved because of their optimism and refusal to consider any other option. I am sure in our own personal experiences, anyone of us will have no difficulty in identifying many examples of successful people whose singular quality was an abundant supply of optimism. In some ways it is the essential oil which lubricates the machine of hope. Without this driving force and inexhaustible source of energy little will be achieved even under the best conditions.

Over the years in both my private and professional career, I have had the good fortune to meet with, or read about a large number of people who have displayed by word, deed or example varying degrees of optimism in their lives. Many of them I have admired, and in some cases I have tried to emulate in my own life. But of all of these, there is one person who for me, stands out as a phenomenal example of the power of optimism in determining the quality of life and living.

I refer to the incomparable *Helen Adam Keller,* the renowned American author, political activist and lecturer, who was able to overcome a profound handicap of deaf/blindness which she acquired from early childhood following an acute infectious disease. With the special help of her teacher, Anne Sullivan, and with determination, fortitude and persistence, she was able to acquire extensive skills in communication and learning, attended Radcliffe College and go on to become a successful advocate for several causes, worldwide. She wrote several well received books and in her lifetime received international recognition in America, Europe and Asia.

Throughout her life, Helen Keller attributed her own accomplishments to her profound optimism and did not hesitate to demonstrate this in word, deed or action. From very early in her life, she resolved to make the most of her life and not let any circumstance, handicap or other misfortune to determine her fate. In fact she firmly believed that lessons can be learnt even in these situations. In 1903, while still an undergraduate at Radcliffe, she published a short essay entitled *The Optimist,* in which she expressed her feelings on this subject. It is a masterpiece and should be read by everyone*.

For me, I shall always remember Helen Keller not as a person who overcame profound handicaps, but for having left us a legacy of overcoming the obstacles of life by living a life driven by optimism and her belief that:

> *"Optimism is the faith that leads to achievement.*
> *Nothing can be done without hope and confidence"*

*http://www.archive.org/stream/optimismessay00kelliala#page/14/mode

Optimism is a seed grown in the soil of faith.
....William Arthur Ward

Optimism is the foundation of courage.
....Nicholas Murray Butler

Teaching is the greatest act of Optimism.
.....Colleen Wilcox

An Optimist is the man who always sees the glass half full;
-Even in the desert.
.....Edward A. Moses

Optimism is the opium of the people.
.....Milan Kundera

The Optimist sees the rose and not its thorns,
The pessimist stares at the thorns, oblivious of the rose.
....Khalil Gibran.

An Optimist sees an opportunity in every difficulty,
A pessimist sees the difficulty in every opportunity.
....Sir Winston Churchill

An Optimist is a person who travels on nothing,
from nowhere to happiness.
.....Mark Twain

Living with Love,
Lessons from the life of Blessed Teresa of Kolkata

"Well, on that fated morning of their meeting (a morning that would change him for the rest of his life) he met her as she was working out in the streets with sick and poor people in a ghetto like he had never seen before, amid stench, filth, garbage, disease, and poverty that was just unbelievable. But what struck Muggeridge more than anything else, even there in that awful squalor and decadence, was the deep, warm glow on Mother Teresa's face and the deep, warm love in her eyes."

The above quotation taken from the writings of *Rowland Croucher*, relates to the experience of *Thomas Malcolm Muggeridge*, the famous English author, satirist, left wing intellectual and committed life-long agnostic, after an encounter with *Blessed Teresa of Kolkata* about whom he was doing a documentary in 1970. Muggeridge was a formidable figure who commanded prodigious literary and rhetorical skills and the respect of the world's leaders, famous and infamous. He, up to that point, was a dedicated vocal and committed non-religious. Yet, he was so overwhelmed by this experience that subsequently in 1982, at the age of 79 he converted to Catholicism and became a committed disciple of the life and teachings of Jesus Christ. In everything he subsequently wrote or spoke of, he never hesitated to credit this decision directly to this encounter with Mother Teresa.

This experience is by no means unique or unusual. It is but one of many thousands of examples of how this gentle, simple, caring lady of Albanian origin, who was born in a small obscure town in *Macedonia* in 1910 and who from a very early age decided to devote her life in the service of God through caring for the least cared, most helpless and neediest of people. After traveling to various centers including a short stay in Ireland to learn English, she went to India in 1929 and entered the *Convent of Loreto* where she began her novitiate and taught at the school, taking her final vows in 1937. She continued to teach at the school for more than 10 years with great success but felt compelled to do something to alleviate the abject poverty all around her. In 1947, she gave up the security of the convent and the school to *"answer the call to help the poor by living among them"* and began her activities in streets of *Kolkata, India.* By 1950, her efforts were so successful, she founded the *Missionaries of Charity,* and by the time she died in 1997 it had expanded to 123 countries where there were in excess of 600 missions devoted to *the poor, sick, orphaned and dying.* For over 45 years she devoted her life to this service, driven by her love for her fellow man and her service to her God.

Even after she gained international acclaim as a humanitarian and a universal advocate for the poor, the sick and the helpless, and was awarded all the most prestigious awards from nations around the world, she never lost the humility of spirit and the all-consuming love for her God and his people that had been the driving force of her entire life. I personally, can attest to this, as a result of a very brief and fleeting moment of being in her presence. The aura of love and caring that surrounded this beautiful spirit was overpowering and has remained with me for more than 30 years after the episode. Indeed she was someone who had truly found deep and profound peace and was not afraid to share her vision of unconditional love and service.

For me, *Mother Teresa* was the absolute pinnacle of the meaning of pure love. She expressed this simply and most dramatically, in the following terms:

> *"The success of love is in the loving;*
> *- it is not in the result of loving."*

Too often have we all tended, consciously or unconsciously, to associate sharing our love with some kind of reward or gain. We invariably attempt to place a value on it and expect some type of meaningful return. If we show our love to you, them we expect you, at minimum, to acknowledge and appreciate our efforts, and we become upset and disappointed when there is no response. The lesson from Mother Teresa is clear and unambiguous. Love, to be effective, must be given unconditionally, without reservation, with no strings attached and no expectation of response. Anything less than this is not true love and should not be categorized as such.

The Greeks refer to this form of love as *"Agape"*, which literally means *Unconditional Love*, a unique expression that is clearly distinguished by its nature, its character and its intention. It has its strong roots in the bible and its major reference in the words of John 3:16:

> *"For God so loved the world, that he sent his only begotten Son;*
> *That whosoever believes in him, shall never perish,*
> *But have everlasting life."*

If God, in his infinite mercy, is willing to sacrifice his Son, *Jesus Christ*, to save the world, how could there be any greater expression of love?

And how then, could any one who truly believes in God and who is genuinely determined to serve him and his people in need in his holy name can afford to do otherwise?

This is the fundamental reasoning that has sustained and reinforced Mother Teresa's commitment and has driven her to try harder and harder to carry out her vocation. In fact, despite all her amazing record of service and success, there were times when she became despondent and depressed because of her concern that she was not fully complying with God's expectation and that God was displeased with her actions. But to the rest of the world, she will always be respected for the work she performed, the service to the sick and needy she provided, and above all, the message that she taught us all that:

> *"It is not how much we do, but how much love we put in the doing.*
> *It is not how much we give, but how much love we put in the giving."*

QUOTATIONS ON LOVE BY BLESSED TERESA OF KOLKATA

-The greatest science in the world, in heaven and on earth; is love.

-The hunger for love is much more difficult to remove
than the hunger for bread.

-It is not how much you do, but how much Love you put into the doing
that matters.

-Love is repaid by love alone!

-I have found the paradox that if I love until it hurts, then there is no
hurt,
but only more love.

-If you judge people, you have no time to love them.

-Spread love everywhere you go: First of all in your own home.
Give love to your children, to your wife or husband,
to your next door neighbor.

-Love is a fruit in season at all times, and within
the reach of every hand.

-We can do no great things; only small things with great love.

-Spread love everywhere you go. Let no one ever come to you without
leaving happier. -Intense love does not measure, it just gives.

-It is easy to love the people far away. It is not always easy to love
those close to us.

-It is not the magnitude of our actions but the amount of love that is
put into them that matters.

-Do not think that love in order to be genuine has to be extraordinary.
What we need is to love without getting tired. Be faithful in small
things, because it is in them that your strength lies.

-Let us always meet each other with smile,
for the smile is the beginning of love.

-What can you do to promote world peace? Go home and
love your family.
If you think well of others, you will also speak well
of others and to others.
From the abundance of the heart the mouth speaks. If your heart is
full of love, you will speak of love.

The Message not the Messenger

"The Legionaries of Christ, an influential Roman Catholic religious order, have been shaken by new revelations that their founder, who died a year ago, had an affair with at least one woman and fathered a daughter just as he and his thriving conservative order were winning the acclaim of Pope John-Paul II".

This statement reported by *Laurie Goldstein* in the New York Times in February, 2009, referred to the exploits of *Rev. Marcial Maciel Degollado*, the founder of the highly influential order, *The Legion of Christ*, during the period 1940–1970. It is alleged he led a double life that included affairs with several women in which he fathered several children, as well as the molestation and sexual abuse of dozens of young men and women, including his own children, while they were students under his care.

Then there is the recent story of the Catholic priest who, in 1980, took over a mission in Pompano Beach, Florida and within a few short years was able to build a large and thriving community of worshippers and a very successful TV program which had achieved International acclaim. All of this came to an abrupt end after accusations of sexual abuse surfaced involving young men and other priests going back for many years.

In 1988, the highly successful Evangelist, *Jimmy Swaggart,* who had built up a very large and devout following, stirred up a damning controversy after a private investigator found he had solicited a prostitute for sex. Initially, Swaggart denied the accusations publicly, but after irrefutable evidence surfaced, he later confessed and publicly apologized for the acts in what has become a landmark televised broadcast. He has never recovered from this scandal, losing his reputation and his following.

These are but three of endless examples of the failings of human beings who are entrusted with the sacred responsibilities of helping others to navigate through the complex and confusing paths to God's salvation. In the overall context of the very large numbers who have and are, successfully working and guiding the populace, the numbers are miniscule. But when viewed against the impact upon the trusting followers and the resulting effects upon their individual psyches, the damage caused is significant. The extent of suffering, both physical and psychological, caused by these actions in terms of disappointment and disillusionment among such an enormous number of trusting and defenseless followers is substantial. The majority of the victims, because of shame, disappointment or justifiable resentment, will never ever be known or heard from, and most unfortunately, will be cheated from the opportunity of receiving God's promises, through no fault of their own.

The perpetrators deserved to be publicly chastised and where necessary, be punished for their unforgivable transgressions and be removed from their positions of responsibility so that they are prevented from doing further damage. But even as we do this, we must be careful to separate their actions from those of the con-men and charlatans who set themselves up with the deliberate intention of cheating their unsuspecting victims. Their intentions and actions are fraudulent from the start, and should be viewed and treated as such.

However paradoxical it may be, we must be willing to recognize that in respect of the wayward preachers, there is a fundamental and profound difference between the part of person who is inspired to carry out the duties in the name of the Almighty, and the weak and susceptible part that occupies the same body. When you examine the words and the writings of any of these people in their role as evangelist and teacher, without regard to the actions and transgressions committed, you cannot help but be moved by the genuine content and intentions projected, and even more, by the positive effects on the audience.

It takes a special person, or perhaps an inspired person, to influence a large gathering and by their words give hope to those who need it, and rekindle faith in those who are lost, and to do this over and over again. Clearly these people, even as they, in their private lives, behave in unacceptable and despicable ways, are able to do good for many, by delivering a message of hope and salvation. History abounds with examples of people who have succeeded to do a great deal of good while being guilty of personal indiscretions. This should not be surprising since Jesus himself chose sinners to become his disciples with the responsibility to spread the word.

So, as we contemplate the transgressions of these people who are entrusted with the special responsibility of carrying out God's work on earth, let us never forget that, like us all, they are sinners and capable of committing sin.

> ....*All the more reason that we never ever forget to concentrate on "<u>The Message</u>" they deliver, and not on the "<u>The Messengers</u>" who deliver it.*

Living with Memories

*R*ecently I had the most satisfying and rewarding experience of meeting with a colleague whom I had last seen fifty two years ago when
we both graduated from Medical School. Although we had not seen or com-
municated with each other for all this while, it was amazing how readily the
memories of that period came flowing back and how easy we were able to recall
events that had taken place so many years ago. In over the short span of a few
hours we were able to restore and recall encounters, faces and events that had
laid buried in our memory banks for so many years, and experience emotions
that had remained dormant for just as long. For a brief period I was young again,
reliving the past, savoring the faces and the visions of people and places I had not
seen for more than five decades. Most importantly, I was again feeling the emotions that once dominated my life and had remained buried for all these years by
all my subsequent life experiences.

The following quotation is taken from one of the episodes of the popular television show *"The Wonder Years"*, which appeared on ABC during 1988 to
1993.

> *"Memory is a way of holding onto the things you love,*
> *the things you are, the things you never want to lose".*

To me this epitomizes the basic meaning of memories of a time gone by. They
play a very fundamental role in the lives of every one of us. It is through our
memories that we learn to live and to acquire skills and learn to avoid dangers.
It is by remembering events in our lives and the outcomes of these events that
we learn and acquire new skills. And equally, it is by remembering our mistakes

and errors that we learn to correct ourselves. In these ways memories serve to define us as who we are and who we strive to be. In the end, it is only by remembering what we, or others, have done or did not do, can we learn who we truly are or want to be.

But memories are very subjective and unless we are careful, they can become distorted over time by our attitudes and interpretations. Most of us have a tendency to take for granted the reliability of our memory and to assume that it will always serve us well. The truth is that even in optimum conditions we generally remember only those things we want to remember or that have impacted us, positively or negatively, in a significant way. I am sure we can all attest to instances where our memory of an event or situation is colored more by its effect on us than by the actual occurrence. We tend to suppress anything which may cause us pain or disappointment so much that, when it is recalled later, much of it is erased. Extensive research has confirmed the unreliability and inconsistency of memory in accurately recording and reproducing an event. So much depends on the individual, his state of mind and the prevailing conditions, that we should all be very careful when giving total credence to a memory.

That not withstanding, memories occupy a very important and integral part of our lives and there is very little that we do that does not involve the use, in one way or another, of our memory. From the moment of waking and throughout the day all our thoughts, actions or decisions are subject to, and under the influence of our memories. We choose what we wear, or what we eat or what we say by referring to our past memory and then deciding. The more complex the decision, the more dependent we are on our ability to process information from our memory banks. In fact in some ways, the fundamental difference between average and intelligent behavior is the ability to efficiently process our memories.

It should be no surprise that anything which interferes with our memories will profoundly affect our behavior. We see this in a reversible form following the use of alcohol, drugs and in clinical toxic states. We see it also in its most tragic and painful manifestation in the chronic brain disorders associated with Alzheimer's Dementia or Stroke's where we witness the progressive disintegration of the brain tissue. Anyone who has had to spend sometime taking care of such people will be forever traumatized by the appalling damage resulting from the loss of the memory systems. These diseases underline the classical effect of the power of memory in our lives and the supreme tragedy that occurs when it is lost.

Charles Baudelaire, the eminent nineteenth century French poet and critic, who was often described as being antisocial, antireligious, antiestablishment and spent his life living that way, most eloquently described this tragedy in his own life as he slowly recognized his brain being progressively consumed with Syphilis contracted as a young man:

> *"How little remains of the man I once was;-save the memory of him!*
> *But then remembering is only a new form of suffering".*
>
> *--Tragically, it does not require any stretch of imagination to recognize*
> *that any one of us is but one incident away from this happening to us.*

> *Memories are the treasures locked deep within the storehouse of our*
> *souls;*
> *To keep our hearts warm when we are lonely.*
> *.......Becky Aligada*

> *Take care of all your memories.*
> *You cannot relive them.*
> *.....Bob Dylan*

> *It doesn't matter who my father was;*
> *It matters who I remember he was.*
> *.....Ann Sexton*

We must always keep old memories,
and young hopes.
......*Arsene Houssave*

Our memories are the only paradise,
From which we cannot be expelled.
.....*Jean-Paul Richter*

It's surprising how much memory is built
around things unnoticed at the time.
........*Barbara Kingsolver*

Anyone who limits her vision to memories of yesterday,
is already dead.
........*Lillie Langtry*

Nothing fixes a thing so intensely in the memory
as the wish to forget it.
......*Michel de Montaigne*

Memories, pressed between the pages of my mind
Memories, sweetened thru the ages just like wine
......*Elvis Presley*

SECTION 5

Life and Society

Society consists of a group of people sharing common social, cultural and economic ideals and relationships.

The individual within the Society is required to conform to certain norms, but otherwise is free to function within it as he sees fit.

We learn from the experiences of others within the society and fashion our lives to conform.

When, for whatever reason this does not happen then problems arise and society becomes intolerant.

What Goes Around Comes Around
A Story of Helping, Rewarding and Gratitude

*T*his story which has, over the years, appeared in a variety of forms may or may not be accurate. The message it projects however is very true and for this reason and if for no other reason, is worth retelling. It is presented in its original form without comment because no comment is necessary:

His name was Fleming, and he was a poor Scottish farmer. One day, while trying to eke out a living for his family, he heard a cry for help coming from a nearby bog. He dropped his tools and ran to the bog. There, mired to his waist in black muck, was a terrified boy, screaming and struggling to free himself. Farmer Fleming saved the lad from what could have been a slow and terrifying death.

The next day, a fancy carriage pulled up to the Scotsman's sparse surroundings. An elegantly dressed nobleman stepped out and introduced himself as the father of the boy Farmer Fleming had saved. *"I want to repay you,"* said the nobleman. *"You saved my son's life."* *"No, I can't accept payment for what I did,"* the Scottish farmer replied, waving off the offer. At that moment, the farmer's own son came to the door of the family hovel.

"Is that your son?" the nobleman asked.

"Yes," the farmer replied proudly.

"I'll make you a deal. Let me take him and give him a good education. If the lad is anything like his father, he'll grow to a man you can be proud of."

And that he did. In time, Farmer Fleming's son graduated from St. Mary's Hospital Medical School in London, and went on to become known throughout the world as the famous, Nobel award winning, Sir Alexander Fleming, the discoverer of Penicillin.

Years afterward, the nobleman's son was stricken with pneumonia. His life was saved by Penicillin. The name of the nobleman was Lord Randolph Churchill and his son's name was Winston.

Confirming, yet again, the often repeated statement:

"WHAT GOES AROUND COMES AROUND."

Life with Miracles
A personal view.

There are only two ways to live your life;
One is as though nothing is a Miracle.
The other is as though everything is a Miracle.

This statement recorded by Albert Einstein, the great German-American theoretical physicist, philosopher and author, universally regarded as one of the world's most influential and best known scientists, encapsulates to me, by its clarity and simplicity, the true status of Miracles in our society. Where many of his scientific collegues denied the existence of a Supreme Being, and insisted that all of nature and its laws can be explained on the basis of predictable evolution, he held firmly to the belief that the universe had to be the work of a supernatural entity. He expressed this view thus:

> *"Every one who is seriously involved in the pursuit of science becomes convinced that a spirit is manifest in the laws of the Universe. A spirit vastly superior to that of man, and one, in the face of which, we, with our modest powers, must feel humble."*

To him, life itself was a miracle. He did not feel that he needed to explain or define those events that cannot be explained by the known laws of nature. He had no difficulty in assigning these occurrences to either the result of our incomplete knowledge, or to a "superior spirit". But Einstein, and others like the great Portuguese Philosopher Spinoza and many of the world great scientists, while accepting the existence of a superior spirit, was unwilling to accept the concept of a Personal God and all that this implies. To me this view is unfortunate and incomplete, for one does not need to witness a miracle to believe in a God of miracles. Although I have never witnessed a true miracle in my lifetime, I believe firmly, that they do occur and that they are the work of an Almighty God and that they appear as part of a Divine Plan.

In strict scientific terms, Miracles are defined as events which occur as a result of the "divine" intervention of some supernatural entity or outside force, must survive rigorous scrutiny and must fulfill rigid criteria. History is replete with records of miracles that have occurred and of their impact on the society. All the great religions, past and present, have acknowledged their existence and have given them prominent positions in their literature. Miracles play a central role in the Christian churches, in Islam and in Judaism. The New and Old Testament of the Holy Bible, the Holy Koran and the Talmud contain an abundance of references of events that are true miracles.

Many of the great philosophers and thinkers have spent their lives in searching and understanding these events. A study of any of these miracles readily reveals clear evidence of divine intervention as an intention or fulfillment of a purpose. There is no evidence that these are indiscriminate, random or purposeless occurrences but rather the deliberate work of the Almighty God over his domain. But we do not need to witness such miracles to be convinced of God's presence or power. St. Augustine of Hippo, the great philosopher and Christian theologian who lived in the 4th century AD, expressed this view most eloquently in the following quotation:

Miracles are not contrary to nature;
But only contrary to what we know of nature.

But Miracle also has a casual usage which is an important fundamental component to life and living. It is often used in the context of a variety of unusual events occurring most often with a beneficial outcome that was hoped for but not expected. We can all relate to these and when they occur they are accepted as such, without giving rise to doubt or challenge. Such occurrences, like surviving a natural disaster, or a life-threatening situation, or avoiding a harmful outcome, or receiving unexpected good news are viewed as evidence of "the hand of the Almighty at work" and more or less accepted by all but the most skeptical among us. Deepak Chopra, the Indian-American Physician and Public Speaker, was speaking for every believer when he expressed his views as follows:

> *"Miracles happen every day.*
> *Not just in remote country villages,*
> *Nor at holy sites halfway across the globe,*
> *But here, in our own lives".*

Over the many years of my life, both professional and personal, I have witnessed and can attest to a large number of events which have left me in awe, without a reason or an explanation. Some are striking and dramatic as was the case of a young man not quite 29 years old, diagnosed with Acute Lymphocytic Leukemia who was told by a highly respected Oncologist that his prognosis was very guarded and not likely to exceed 6 months, yet was alive and well ten years after. Or the severe post-traumatic accident victim who regained consciousness more than 18 months after the accident and went on to lead a full life, or the case of a 67 year old man who received a direct lightening strike while playing golf, was completely knocked out and apparently in cardiac arrest, yet got up shortly after and went home unaided. But stunning as these may be, they are but a small part of the miracles of life around us.

At this point in my life I share the view of many, that life itself is the miracle. Their existence can be seen more as a measure of the extent of the acceptance and beliefs of individual than on any scientific exposure. In the end the final decision as to the existence and acceptance of miracles will always be left to the individual. As Nancy Gibbs, the author, commentator and editor for TIME magazine, so eloquently observed:

> *"For the truly faithful, no Miracle is necessary.*
> *For those who doubt, no Miracle is sufficient".*

< >

To be alive, to be able to see, to walk;
…….. It's all a Miracle.
…..Arthur Rubinstein

Miracles happen to those who believe in them.
……….Bernard Berenson

Nobody sees the obvious, nobody observes the ordinary.
There are more miracles in a square yard of earth
than in all the fables of the Church.
………Robert Anton Wilson

Once all struggles is grasped, miracles are possible.
….Mao Tse-Tung

The Seven Golden Rules of Life

One of the most popular and extremely widely distributed publications is a list of quotations entitled <u>The Seven Golden Rules of Life</u>. Its origin or authors have never been definitively identified, but its content is, to my mind, a rich collection of wise and insightful advice worthy of serious consideration by all. They have always attracted my attention and encouraged me to seek out a meaning for each one as they relate to my own life situation. The following comments are strictly my own personal interpretations and are offered with the hope that you may be encouraged to search out you own positions. I am sure you will find the exercise as rewarding as I did.

<u>RULE1:</u> <u>TRUE RELATIONSHIPS</u>

> *"Don't let someone become a priority in your life,*
> *When you are just an option in their life;*
> *Relationships work best when they are balanced."*

True, meaningful relationships are the foundation of a rich and rewarding life. As human beings our lives are based on a continuous interaction with others. In our day-to-day life we are constantly relating with others, whether this be in the school, work-place, social environment or at home. The great majority of these encounters are generally superficial, serve to satisfy an immediate need or situation and then quickly fade from memory or consciousness upon completion, without any lasting effect. These are the tools of daily living that we all must acquire and implement in order to continue living.

But in addition to this, we all need and search out people with whom we can develop deeper and more meaningful relationships. The types that are based on trust, tolerance, acceptance and mutual respect. Without these, our lives will be robbed of the fulfillment and richness that only comes from a relationship where honesty, respect and understanding can provide a quality that rises above all other encounters. However, the term "meaningful relationship" is very subjective and obviously can be interpreted differently by different individuals. It will also vary from time to time, depending on such factors as age, circumstances and state of mind.

But whatever the prevailing conditions, the one constant factor which determines the depth and strength of any such relationship is the bond which holds the relationship together. If this bond is lopsided, if it is based on anything but a full and equal interaction it will neither grow nor even survive. Such a relationship, to become truly successful, must indeed be completely balanced, where each party contributes to their fullest and where the sum total of the contributions adds up to 100%. It certainly does not necessarily or absolutely require *equal* participation, but rather *total* participation. Under these circumstances the quality of relationship is as rewarding as it is lasting. It gives joy to life and reason for living.

RULE 2:   KNOW YOURSELF

> *Never explain yourself to anyone.*
> *Because the person who likes you doesn't need it,*
> *and the person who dislikes you won't believe it.*

This rule relates specifically to the need for you to know yourself, to know who you are, and to avoid the temptation to measure yourself with other people's yardsticks.

Much has been written and spoken about this rule and there are volumes of confusing opinions expressed as to its real meaning. Some opinions see this as a *"matter of power and control"* where, by explaining yourself, you risk loss of control and hand authority over you to another party. Yet others have suggested that any attempt to explain your action implies a subconscious *feeling of uncertainty and inferiority and a desire for positive feedback* at all cost.

I do not believe either of these explanations is complete. My personal view is more fundamental and not as complicated. I do not believe that I need to prove anything to any one but myself to justify this rule. As I see it, it is a statement of fact which does not need an explanation. Those people who know and like me, will already have sought out the needed information about me and will have formed a favorable opinion and a level of trust.

On the other hand, for those who, for whatever reason, have an unfavorable opinion, no amount of explanation will be necessarily persuasive. In the end therefore, you are ultimately answerable to yourself alone, and you ought to be guided solely by this principle in all things. *William Shakespeare* brilliantly described this principle in *Hamlet, act 1,* thus:

> *"Above all, to your own self be true,*
> *and it must follow, as the night the day,*
> *You cannot then be false to any man."*

RULE 3: MAKING EXCUSES

> *When you keep saying you are too busy, then you are never free.*
> *When you keep saying you have no time, then you will never have time.*
> *When you keep saying you will do it tomorrow,*
> *then tomorrow will never come.*

One of the major failings of human behavior is the problem of procrastination. It seems that, unlike any other member of the animal kingdom, we are endowed with this tendency to make excuses. It seems that throughout our lifetime we spend more time and effort in the art of avoiding or postponing actions, often at our ultimate disadvantage.

As I see it, our use of excuses is related to our reluctance to accept responsibility for our actions, or more precisely, our reluctance to accept the failures that can result from our actions. The problem is that as we continue to make excuses we begin to believe them and pretty soon they become self-fulfilling prophesies. When we believe we are too busy, then clearly we will never be free to find ourselves. And if we think there is no time available then we will never find the time to explore our opportunities. When we are convinced there is no tomorrow, then it does not make sense to plan for the future.

We have to realize that excuses, however they appear, will negate responsibility and encourage procrastination. By recognizing and refusing to make excuses and accepting responsibility for all our actions we inevitably reap the rewards of success, whether this be personal self-respect, or trust and acceptance by others or confidence to move forward. This indeed, is the fundamental difference between success and failure!

Dr. Benjamin Franklin, a leading American author, inventor, politician and statesman, one of the Founding Fathers of the United States of America, effectively summarized this outcome in the following manner:

"He that is good for making excuses is seldom good for anything else."

RULE 4: GIFT OF CHOICES

When we wake up in the morning, we have two simple choices;
Go back to sleep and dream on, or wake up and chase our dreams.

One of life's greatest gifts and the single most important difference between Human Beings and the rest of the Animal Kingdom is the freedom of choice. The ability to choose a specific course of action from a set of alternatives is as much a blessing as it is a curse. Unlike the animal whose choice is strictly limited to the demands for its survival, we have been granted the wonderful opportunity of achieving goals based on circumstances far beyond immediate gratification, that permit us to plan into the future.

This gift of choice does not automatically guarantee happiness or success, and certainly does not ensure special benefits for the individual. These will only come when we exercise the right options and make the right decisions.

This freedom to choose is the fundamental engine of life and the creative force for living. But it comes with certain individual responsibilities which require us to take action. If we do nothing, we get back nothing in return. If on the other hand we accept the responsibility and act accordingly, then each choice will be rewarded and will lead on to further choices. This is, in the most basic sense, the true meaning of life. *We are indeed the product of our choices!*

RULE 5: CARING ABOUT OTHERS

> *"We make them cry, who care for us.*
> *We cry for those, who never care for us.*
> *And we care for those, who will never cry for us.*
> *…..This is the truth of life, strange but true.*
> *Once you realize this, it's never too late to change."*

One of the unfortunate failings of the human mind is the unpredictable response to emotional situations. By and large our reactions are impulsive responses without due regard to the circumstances. This often leads to inappropriate responses and opens one to the opportunity of potential exploitation. Under those circumstances, we tend to make the wrong decisions and expect to achieve the right outcomes.

The irony of this truth is that we are all fully aware of its existence but we rarely ever make any effort to correct the situation. This leads to the unhappy outcome of favoring those who have no care for us and taking for granted the good of those who truly care for us. This paradox of behavior is related to a large extent to the influence of our environment which is directed to appeasement at all cost, without due regard to the effect on ourselves.

In the end, we must recognize that this a fact of life and we will do well always guard against it. By making every effort to identify those who really care for us and give them the recognition they deserve, even as we continue to care for all others, friends or foe alike. This will go a long way to secure peace and happiness in us.

RULE 6: CHOOSING TO ACT

Don't make promises when you are in joy.
Don't reply when you are sad.
Don't make decisions when you are angry.
Think twice before you act.

One of the major shortcomings of many of us is the constant inconsistency of our responses. In our haste to please others, or our urge to protect ourselves while retaining good feelings we tend to make decisions without regard to prevailing conditions, only to regret it later.

It makes good sense to avoid responding or reacting decisively whenever we are under the influence of any kind of emotional state since our decision is likely to be more impulsive than reasonable. We run the risk of regretting later, a decision which is spoken in haste at an inappropriate time. Hence the advice to *think twice* before acting is so important. By doing so we avoid a great deal of unnecessary pain!

Bob Dylan, one of the foremost exponents of American folk music, summarized this problem in the following words:

"People seldom do what they believe in.
-They do what is convenient, and then regret."

RULE 7: LIVE YOUR LIFE

"Time is like a river. You cannot touch the same water twice,
since the flow that has passed, will never pass again.
….Enjoy every moment of your life today!"

For as long as I can recall I have been taught the concept that *time is like a flowing river whose waters, once passed will never pass again.* The great English physicist *Stephen Hawkings* expanded this concept to include life, itself, which he describes

as "*like a river on which it seems that each of us are carried relentlessly by its current.*" -
Time is indeed the master of life!

To me the message is as loud as it is clear. As our life, like time, flows
relentlessly forward, it is incumbent on us to make use of every opportunity
to seek enrichment and satisfaction in our lives and our environment. So often
we overlook many opportunities or avoid challenges, or ignore chances for so
many foolish and illogical excuses, when in fact, had we moved appropriately,
the result would have been rewarding.

Instead of measuring our success by a series of disjointed, isolated and acci-
dental incidents, it would be so much better if we remain alert and prepared to
make use of every opportunity as it comes along the flowing river. In this way,
rather than waiting for others and losing the opportunity, we will have the joy
and satisfaction of success and avoid the need to embark on the frustrating act
of following them after they have passed on. This is indeed the fundamental difference between success and failure.

Leonardo da Vinci, the great Italian painter and social philosopher was truly
insightful when he observed that:

"*Time stays long enough, for anyone who will use it.*"

Life at Christmas

"You who bring good tidings to Jerusalem,
Lift up your voice with a shout, lift it up and do not be afraid;
Say to the towns of Judah: "Here is your God!""

This statement, taken from *Isaiah 40:9,* encapsulates the true meaning of the wonderful season of Christmas. A period set aside for all true Christians to rejoice at the birth of Jesus Christ, the Savior.

Unfortunately, Christmas is becoming increasingly buried by a rising tide of secularism and commercialization. It is rapidly losing whatever religious meaning it ever had, and instead, is becoming just one more excuse for corporations to sell more things. Massive traffic jams, packed shopping malls, and lines stretching around the block have become hallmarks of the holiday season. Even uglier, are the "special sales" used to herald the start of season earlier and earlier that regularly lead to pandemonium and chaos. All of this deliberately designed by the corporations, banks and credit card companies to convince us to spend more and more and owe more and more.

For me however, as I grow older Christmas is a time for my family and myself. The powerful feeling of family is never any stronger than at midnight of Christmas-eve when, gathered with all my family, we welcome together with all the faithful of the Christian world, the glad and glorious tidings of the birth of our Lord. But Christmas is more than just an opportunity for family to gather together and share the joy and love of one another. It is an opportunity for us all to take the time and reflect upon the message of the season, as announced by the angels to the shepherds on that fateful night in *Luke 2:14:*

200

*"Glory to God in the highest,
And on earth, peace and good will toward men"*

Unfortunately, in the same way we have exploited this opportunity to distort and commercialize Christmas, we have also successfully buried this beautiful command from God of *"Peace on earth and Goodwill to all men"* in the mud of exploitation. As we enter this season, instead of *peace on earth,* we have wars raging in every corner of the world and among every nation and even within nations. In fact peace appears to be the most elusive commodity in the whole world.   So too are our leaders, irrespective of whether we elect them or otherwise. We grant the prestigious Nobel Peace Prize upon one of our Presidents and he promptly increases the size and extent of the war in Afghanistan. We are spending more money on building greater and greater weapons than we are feeding and housing our neighbors. We have clearly not learnt any lessons from the past wars and conflicts, nor do we seem to give more than lip service to the mounting death toll and worse still, the mounting numbers of young men and women whose horrendous injuries are an abomination to humanity. --- *And we do this all, in the name of freedom and democracy!*

And as to *goodwill to all men;* few of us have taken the time to understand its true meaning. We appear to prefer the most successful, the most notorious and the most aggressive people as the ones deserving the recognition. We happily appoint a man of very questionable morals as the world's greatest sportsman, a woman of equally questionable character as the greatest entertainer, showering them with our money and adoration. Yet we ignore the millions of people who go from one day to another not knowing if food is available to feed their children.

Even worse than this, is the lopsided attitude of our governments towards the care and support of society. We unhesitatingly spend billions of dollars to support the greedy incompetence of our financial leaders, including handsomely rewarding them with large bonuses for destroying the world's economies. Yet we do not raise a finger to help the increasing pool of our friends and neighbors forced into failure and bankruptcy. *Where in God's name, is the goodwill toward men?*

So as we enter this season of Christmas, a season chosen by God to remind us of our own responsibility towards our brothers and our neighbors let us all commit to live by his words. That we will all strive, by word and by deed, to ensure *peace on earth,* and do whatever and whenever we can, all that we are capable of doing to restoring *good- will toward men.*

God walked down the stairs of heaven with a Baby in His arms.
......Paul Scherer

There has been only one Christmas; The rest are anniversaries.
.......W.J. Cameron

It is Christmas in the heart that puts Christmas in the air.
....W. T. Ellis

May your Christmas be as peaceful and as bright as new fallen snow.
.....Author Unknown

I will honor Christmas in my heart, and keep it all year.
......Charles Dickens

He who has not Christmas in his heart will never find it under a tree.
.... Roy L. Smith

The message of Christmas is that the visible material
world is bound to the invisible spiritual world.
......Author Unknown

What is Christmas? It is tenderness for the past, courage for the
present, hope for the future. It is a fervent wish that every cup may
overflow with blessings rich and eternal, and that every
path may lead to peace.
.......Agnes M. Pharo

The only blind person at Christmastime is;
he who has not Christmas in his heart.
......Helen Keller

Christ was born in the first century, yet he belongs to all centuries.
He was born a Jew, yet He belongs to all races.
He was born in Bethlehem, yet He belongs to all countries.
........George W. Truett

The Butterfly Effect

*F*or as long as I can recall, the Butterfly has been a source of wonder and fascination to me. Not only for its beauty and graceful appearance but equally, its freedom to do whatever it chooses and go wherever it wants. As a student in Trinidad and Tobago where the varieties of butterfly are more than 120 and where the world comes to study them, I spent many hours happily following and trying to catch them. Many years later I attended a lecture while a student at the University in England entitled "Butterfly Effect Theory" in the context of the famous quotation from Edward Lorentz:

"The Fluttering of a Butterfly's wings can affect
climate changes on the other side of the planet"

The speaker explained that in the same way the small wings of a butterfly when used correctly can change weather conditions worldwide, even cause hurricanes or change their direction, so also can anyone of us, at the right time, affect the lives of those around us or even far beyond, for good or for bad. He then went on to stress the importance of making the right choices during our growth and development and equally, avoiding the wrong ones, to ensure our metamorphosis to our full potential.

I have often reflected on the butterfly's lifecycle. This to me represented a true microcosm of life as it should be. It undergoes a transformation from a clumsy, ugly, helpless caterpillar, through being trapped in a cocoon and finally emerging a beautiful, delicate-winged creature capable of changing the world. It models exactly our own cycle of life. We too, must undergo a transformation from the complete confinement of the uterus, the clumsiness and total dependence of childhood and through a period of restrictive, controlled adolescence to emerge as proud confident adults.

I am sure we can all recall times in our lives when we have had to face situations which made us feel as small as a butterfly, convinced that the little we can do will make almost no difference to the lives of those around us. Little did we realize that some times what we do may truly result in significant changes in the lives of people around us and even to those beyond us. These changes would never have happened, had we not taken the initiative to step forward in good faith.

Consider the young Albanian woman called Agnese Gonxhe Bojaxhiu who in 1950 after taking her final vows as a nun, travelled to India to take care of the poor and helpless streetpeople. Later, as *Mother Teresa*, she started a movement that has spread worldwide and continues to administer to millions of the neediest people.

Also the young Scottish physician, *Alexander Fleming,* who discovered the healing properties of the extract of a lowly fungus and subsequently produced the antibiotic Penicillin which has and continues to save many millions of lives.

In both instances dedicated individuals were able to change the lives of innumerable people all over the world without ever knowing who they are.

Quite recently a moving story was featured in one of the CBS evening news broadcasts concerning the life of a very special person, *Chris Rosati*. Even though he is suffering from advanced ALS and is confined to a wheelchair with severely deteriorating speech he continues to try to improve the world around him with random acts of kindness. A short while ago he gave two young girls sitting at the next table to his at a diner $50.00 each with a simple request to "do something kind with it." The incident was forgotten until some time later he received an Email from the people of a small village in Sierra Leone in Africa holding banners that read: *"thanks a lot for spreading kindness – Chris Rosati."* The money was forwarded to the village that had suffered severely from Ebola disease to help the people of the village. Thus proving once again what the impact of a simple act of kindness can have to the people on the other side of the world.

These are but three outstanding examples of the success of the Butterfly Effect that is happening around us daily. If you just reflect a moment, I have no doubt that you too will readily think of many examples in your own life where your action has resulted in benefit to others or alternatively, others have done things that have helped you. If you haven't done so, maybe you should begin to do so. So that the next time you see a butterfly happily fluttering around, you will take time to remember its potential impact on the world and to remind yourself that you too can achieve the same impact if only you open your eyes and your mind to the world.

We delight in the beauty of the Butterfly;
But rarely admit the changes it has gone through
to achieve that beauty.
.....Maya Angelou

Just like the Butterfly, you too will awaken in your own time.
........Deborah Chaskin

I only ask to be free; The Butterflies are free.
......Charles Dickens

I do not know whether I was then a man dreaming I was a Butterfly;
or whether I am now a Butterfly dreaming I am a Man.
........Chuang Tzu (Zhuangzi)

The butterfly counts not months but moments,
and has time enough.
........Rabindranath Tagore

Love is like a butterfly;
It goes where it pleases and it pleases wherever it goes.
...Author unknown

The Fabric of Life

"Life is a network of invisible threads."

The above quotation from the pen of the great Victorian-era English authoress George Eliot is as dramatic as it is simple. Life, to me, is a complex fabric made up of all the threads of experience collected during a whole lifetime. You begin life as a plain cloth made up of the many characteristics you inherited from your parents. It is pure, clean and unadulterated. As you go through life you begin to add threads derived from all the knowledge, experiences, encounters and influences you acquire along the way, resulting in a mosaic of exquisite complexity and specificity. A cursory look at this mosaic will reveal an apparent accumulation of unrelated threads which appear to have been woven together in a random pattern with no regard to sequence or order. Many people will try to convince you that your life is merely the sum total of all your experiences piled up one upon the other, like a layered cake, purely by chance without any reason or meaning.

I do not believe that this is correct. To me, every single thread, as it weaves itself into the mosaic affects, and is affected, by every other thread it encounters. Over its lifetime it is modified by, and it modifies the appearance and texture of the fabric, changing its color, appearance, feel and outlook. And as it does, so are we affected in our attitudes, our expectations, our hopes and our desires. Indeed we become the product of what we are and our behavior is determined by this. Lea Yekutiel, noted Inspirational speaker and author, extended this concept by noting:

> *"The fabric of life, with all the threads interacting together can be quite positive, but if one thread negatively vibrates against another thread or*

is angry because another thread is "in a better place" or "looks better",
the feelings are passed through the whole cloth and is absorbed and
experienced by all."

By natural extension, this principle applies not only to each one of us as individuals but to us as a group, as a society, as a nation and to the world. In a very meaningful way each one of us can and do impact the rest of the world by our actions, positively or negatively. In this context, I am reminded of the concept of "the butterfly effect theory" first postulated in 1963 by the American meteorologist Edward Lorentz with his famous quotation:

"The Fluttering of a Butterfly's wings can affect climate changes
on the other side of the planet"

In the same way that a small insignificant butterfly, by flapping its wings, can affect the climate thousands of miles away, so too can the movement of a single thread affect the fabric of the environment around it. We need only to look around us to see repeated examples of this in our day to day living.

In my own personal life, I have witnessed, like no doubt every one else, many instances where a random encounter has led directly or indirectly, to significant life-changing events for which I am truly grateful. Very often these effects appeared several years after the initial encounter and in ways that could not have been anticipated or predicted. I am indeed the product of all my encounters. I still recall an incident when I was no more than 5 years old and was taken to see Dr. Pau, a kind Chinese physician, for my inflamed leg. His gentle spirit and caring way made me resolve that I too, would like to be a physician. Some 20 years later I recalled that moment as I received my Graduation certificate and was grateful for that original encounter.

As I see it, the Fabric of our life is uniquely our own, to do as we wish. We can choose to abuse it without respect or regard, and then suffer the consequences of pain, regret and eternal damnation. Or to nuture and support it, to respect it and expand it, and in return enjoy the rewards that will inevitably come as we journey along on the road of life;

-- *and beyond.*

Pericles, the outstanding Greek statesman and orator, who lived around 400BC, has described this most eloquently in the following manner:

> *"What you leave behind is not what is engraved in stone monuments,*
> *but what is woven into the Lives of others."*

> *Life is not advancement, it is Growth.*
> *It does not move upwards, but expands in all directions.*
> *........Russell G. Alexander*

> *The art of life lies in a constant readjustment to our surroundings.*
> *.... Okakura Kakuzo*

> *The art of living lies not in eliminating but in growing with troubles.*
> *.....Bernard M. Baruch*

> *The measure of a life, after all, is not its duration, but its donation.*
> *....Corrie Ten Boom*

> *You don't get to choose how you're going to die, or when.*
> *But you can decide how you're going to live now.*
> *......Joan Baez*

> *What is important in life is Life, and not the result of life.*
> *.....Wolfgang Von Goethe*

Exercising Choices
Responding to Adversity

The source of this story is unknown but the message it delivers is strong and very relevant. It applies to every one of us in so many aspects of living that it was felt to be very appropriate under the heading of Life with Choices.

A young woman went to her mother complaining about her life and how things were so hard for her. She did not know how she was going to make it and wanted to give up. She was tired of fighting and struggling. It seemed that as one problem was solved, a new one arose.

Her mother took her to the kitchen. She filled three pots with water and placed each one on a high fire. Soon the water in each pot started to boil. In the first she placed carrots, in the second she placed eggs and in the last one she placed ground coffee beans. She allowed them to continue boiling without saying a word.

After about twenty minutes she turned off the burners. She fished out the carrots and placed them in a bowl. She then pulled the eggs out and placed in another bowl, then ladled the coffee out and placed it into a third bowl. Turning to her daughter she asked, *"Tell me what you see?"*

"Carrots, eggs and coffee" the daughter replied.

Her mother brought her closer and asked her to feel the carrots. She did, and noted that they were soft. The mother then asked her to take an egg, break it and remove the shell. She observed it to be hard boiled. Finally, the mother asked her to sip the coffee. After sipping it, she smiled enjoying the rich aroma of the coffee.

Puzzled, the daughter asked: *"What does all this mean, mother?"*

Her mother explained that this is a *lesson in life*. Each of these objects had faced the same adversity, boiling water and each had reacted differently.

> ----The carrot went in strong, hard and unrelenting, but after being subjected to boiling water came out softened and weak.
>
> ----The egg was fragile and needed the outer shell to protect its liquid interior, but after sitting through the boiling water, it became hardened and dry.
>
> ----The ground coffee beans were unique however, for after they were in the boiling water, they actually changed the water into something more pleasant and acceptable.

After a short pause, she looked at her daughter and slowly asked her: *"When adversity knocks on your door you must be ready to respond.*

How will you?

> *-Will you be a Carrot and whimper?*
> *-Will you be an egg and get stronger?*
> *-Will you be a Coffee Bean and change the water?"*

The young woman got up and with a smile of understanding, thanked her mother and walked out of the kitchen. She now knew what she wanted.

Dare to Live Life

"Ultimately, the fundamental difference between us when we are faced with adversity lies in our willingness to dare or not to dare and for no other reason"

*T*he above statement supposedly attributed to *Gen. Alexander M. Haig Jr.,* the American military leader and elder statesman, can apply to each and every one of us and to everything that we do or do not do in our lives. It calls on each one of us to recognize it's validity in our own way, and to what extent we are prepared to respond and to how much we are prepared to expend.

Almost 2000 years ago, *Lucius Annaeus Seneca,* the great Roman philosopher and statesman, recognized this paradox and the reason why we choose different outcomes when he wrote:

> *"It is not because things are difficult, that we do not Dare,*
> *it is because we do not Dare, that they are difficult."*

That statement is as valid and as appropriate now as it was 2000 years ago. Every one of us can readily think of others whose behavior or attitude toward a special occasion or event has so impressed us that we stand in awe of them. These people were not superhuman nor were they endowed with any special gifts. They came from among us and shared our weaknesses and our strengths. The only difference is that in a very special situation and under very special conditions, they faced and dealt with adversity at a level far above our comfort levels. They dared to rise above their obstacles and live life above and beyond their normal expectations.

Of the very many examples that have crossed my life over the years, three have impressed me and have left indelible imprints on me, each for a different reason;

The first is the renowned theoretical physicist *Stephen William Hawking*, whose contributions to the fields of quantum gravity and cosmology are hailed by the world's community of scientists. In his lifetime, he has opened up our understanding of the origin of the universe and facilitated space study, understanding and exploration.

At the age of 21 years, while still a student at Cambridge University, England, he was diagnosed with a serious neuromuscular disease, Amyotrophic Lateral Sclerosis (ALS). This is a uniformly fatal disease, characterized by progressive paralysis of all the body's muscles leading to total incapacity. Yet despite progressive, relentless and incapacitating deterioration, he continued to lead an active academic life, lecturing all over the world, publishing many original and ground-breaking papers and scholarly books. Amazingly, he was able to lead a full and rewarding personal life. He is married with three children, has traveled to many countries and participated in a range of lifestyle experiences, including traveling into space.

All of this was done while being almost completely paralyzed and confined totally to a wheelchair. He is able to communicate only by using his eyelids and a very sophisticated computer system. Despite this, he continues to combine family life with his teaching and research into theoretical physics with an extensive program of travel and public lectures. To meet this man is awe-inspiring, not only for the brilliance of his mind, but even much more, to witness the way he was able to overcome these gargantuan obstacles with an aura of confidence and optimism, even as he appears as a "crumpled bundle of humanity" with only a flutter of his eyelids to communicate to the world. Indeed his is the story of a man who defiantly faced his obstacles, and dared to live his life to its fullest.

The second is someone with whom I have had a close relationship for most of my life. He is a man who, for as long as I have known him, has been an indefatigably ambitious man who has never flinched from a challenge and very rarely lost anyone of them. By dint of intense personal effort, hard work and an inexhaustible supply of optimism, he has developed a very successful enterprise and an equally enviable reputation. He has earned the highest respect from his community for his Business skills and generous philanthropy.

Recently, as a result of a series of unfortunate accidents and questionable medical management, he suffered a serious neck injury leading to almost complete paralysis of the upper and lower body. and resulting in the development of a total dependence on others and confinement to bed. To any other man, including myself, this would have resulted in such disappointment and antagonism as to precipitate profound anger and resentment. But in this case this did not happen. Instead we witnessed a change that was at once philosophical as it was a genuine acceptance of a "new life". Rather than resentment, there was a genuine desire to adapt and to accommodate, and instead of anger, there was an urgent effort to learn so that he could teach others by example and experience. Here again, is a unique example of a man who refused to succumb to life-changing adversity and instead, grabbed it with both hands and dared to live his new life to the fullest.

The third person's story came to my attention following the publication of his autobiography entitled "Ghost Boy" a few years ago. It recalls the account of a young man who suffered a life shattering disease at the age of twelve years causing him to gradually lose control of his body and finally falling into a coma at age sixteen. He subsequently began to show gradual recovery of consciousness but not function, so that by age nineteen he was fully conscious, apparently totally aware of his surroundings but unable to communicate. At least this was the assumption for a long time until an alert caregiver recognized that he used his eyes to respond to her and to indicate that he understood. It was only then that corrective action was started. He was provided with a specially adapted speech computer which allowed him to communicate with others. Over the succeeding years he was able to gain further improvement in function so much so that he was able to complete his education, get married and start work. Despite this traumatic experience, this young man has shown great courage and sensitivity without any regret, and as *Catherine Deveney*, an author and journalist, described in an article in *The Scotsman Newspaper* in 2011:

> "His levels of empathy are remarkable, perhaps because he was forced
> for so many years into the role of watcher and listener, hearing people
> unburden their problems around him absorbing their pain without them
> knowing. His communication is strikingly direct, almost fearless in the
> way he confronts emotional reality."

These are but three examples of thousands that exist around us. They are individually inspiring to us as witnesses of the events and induce in us a sense of awe and disbelief, but to the individuals, they are merely natural responses to the circumstances of life.

Someone, whose name I do not recall, once wrote:

> *"It's not the tragedy; it's how we deal with it. It's whether we come out stronger because of it. It's not about blocking out the pain or hiding from it, it's about letting the pain shape you into someone better than you were before."*

This indeed is the true test of our characters and the fundamental differences among us. It is when we are faced with adversity and we are called upon to deal with it that our true character comes out. No one ever said life was easy or fair and none ever promised a bed of roses free from thorns, but we all have within us the ability to overcome these obstacles. The question is whether we choose to make the effort, to dare, to face them!

In this context we should recognize that this ability is by no means unique to just the few successful people but available to all. Throughout the ages, the single most consistent attribute among all who have set out to achieve and succeeded to do so, is the willingness to face difficulties and dare to overcome them at all cost. We see this every day, in every situation and it involves everybody. The only consistent ingredient necessary in every instant is the recognition that, with the right spirit and a willingness to overcome failure, any thing can be achieved. The late *Robert F. Kennedy,* American Senator and Attorney-General, summarized this most eloquently when he wrote:

> *"Only those who dare to fail greatly can ever achieve greatly."*

-No greater advice than this can ever be given!

In Search of the Butterfly
A Short Story of a Young Man's Quest

On the beautiful sunny island in the middle of the day the young man lay
prostrate on the dry, stony bank of the flowing river; his eyes glistened
from the steady tears that trickled down his sad and convoluted face. This was
indeed a low moment in his short and as yet, unfulfilled life. He had already
passed one and one half score in years and had nothing tangible to show, except,
an Apartment of his own, two Dogs and a new car. His faith was surely under
siege but he remained steadfast in his resolve. Over and over he repeated the
battle cry which had served to sustain the black slaves of the south in their
moments of despair and which he had adopted as his own;

"I shall overcome, some day, some day."

Day by day, he had faced slings and barbs from his closest family. His mother,
whom he dearly loved, had recently adopted the "poor-me" approach. Whenever
he was present, she will immediately become morose, depressed and withdrawn, go directly to her bed clutching her bible and repeat over and over;

"Why are you doing this to me my Lord?
What have I done to deserve this punishment?"

The father, not to be outdone, displayed, in no uncertain manner, his absolute
contempt and painful disappointment. With his classic, bone-chilling demeanor,
he had adopted a degree of shearing sarcasm that rivaled the true masters. As
soon as the young man appeared, he would quickly transform his posture in

216

such a manner as to leave no doubt about his displeasure. He compounded this unbearable agony with a total absence of even the slightest acknowledgement of the yeoman effort delivered by the young man. Although he received constant congratulations from all his peers for the son's conduct of the business, he never ever acknowledged his contributions. He would rather give praise to his paid employees, often acknowledging Irene, Jaime or even Dwight, constantly showering unsolicited praise upon them.

All of this was done as part of an elaborate scheme, planned and developed by his wife, to stimulate this young man to "action." She was in fact very experienced in this activity; not only as a result of her *peculiar genetic constitution*, but also from her several past experiences in such matters. For it is well known that as a seventeen year old she successfully planned, developed, initiated and implemented a coup to secure her unsuspecting husband-to-be. The ultimate result was that he succumbed into a state of total mesmerism. Even to this day he remains "bazoodied" in her presence.

One day, as the young man sought refuge on the bank of the river, there came upon him a "visitation". Instantly he recognized the true import of this visit as he recalled the words of the wise old man, whom he knew only as "*Papa Da*" and frequently visited to seek comfort and counsel. The old man would provide support, advice and encouragement, and would always remind him that he must prepare himself for the "visitation". When pressed, he would always add;

> "*You will know when it comes by the sound of the wind.*
> *Just listen for the sound*".

The memory of this day is indelibly etched in the depth of his soul and remains as vivid now, as he replays the events in his mind's eye, as they did at the fateful moment of occurrence. No doubt they will continue to remain as crisp, in perpetuity, passing on from generation to generation.

In the solace of his den and under the influence of a small amount of "Mother Mary" he had drifted into a self induced hypnotic state in the manner taught to him by *Papa Da*. As he entered the "*place of secure enchantment*", he became aware of a soothing, gentle breeze blowing across his face. It was so gentle yet awesome, so quiet yet as thunderous as a booming cannon, so sweet, yet as overpowering as the finest perfume.

With the breeze, he became aware of a sound, quite unlike anything he had heard before. Although he knew better, it felt as if he was at The "Royal Vic" listening to the greatest rendition ever, of "Handel's Messiah" by the London Symphony Orchestra, or at the "Royal Albert Hall" enjoying the solo renditions of Joan Baez at her very best. His heart was racing, trying desperately to keep up with his screaming mind, but never quite catching up. His body felt as if he was deeply immersed inside the bowels an active "Mt. Kilimanjaro", but he knew this was not so, for he was cool to touch.

He knew instinctively that this was indeed the "visitation" promised by *Papa Da*. He also knew that the time was at hand and that, ready or not, his life was about to undergo a significant metamorphosis.

The moment had indeed arrived. The culmination of a long and tortuous journey that took him to the far corners of the world, crossing continents, time zones, oceans and islands. Meeting and exploring peoples, cultures, attitudes and appearances. Studying genetics and genealogy, likes and dislikes, family and non-family, and yet finding nothing but disappointment, and his mother's frustrations. This was more than he could handle. But for the steadfast support of *Papa Da*, he surely would have succumbed to the machinations of his mother and settled down with a *"nice family girl."*

At that fleeting instant he became aware of an vision of the most beautiful butterfly he had experienced. It fluttered gently and gracefully around his face and as it did so, he was overwhelmed with an indescribable sensation of sheer joy and surrender. He recalled it was not unlike the feelings he experienced when he opened the bottle of pure, extra distilled, Vintage Virgin Olive Oil extracted from the first crop of olives harvested from the sacred Olive Groves situated at the foothills of Mount Olive in the ancient hills of Lebanon, offered as a special gift to his father. Suddenly, he was overcome with the desire to search out this butterfly, to gently caress its beauty and take her home to meet his mother.

He woke up with a start, he must find the butterfly, but except for the Olive Grove, he had no idea of how to begin. He thought that he may have to visit Lebanon and search the sacred groves. But that was not easy to do and there was no guaranty of success. The vision consumed his every moment. He was driven to solve this dilemma. His parents were not helpful. His father questioned whether he was on "crack". His mother a devout Roman Catholic said that she would speak to Fr. Mullen who knew everything and also advised him to go to confession and to daily morning mass.

Papa Da on the other hand, was not surprised. In fact he was expecting this news, for had he not spoken to him in the past and advised him to listen for the "sound". Taking hold of the young man's hands, the old man guided him to a special garden with a gentle stream and a pond filled with the most beautiful Koi fish he had ever seen. He closed his eyes, paused for a brief moment and then spoke thus:

> *"Young man, you must never forget that;*
> *The most exquisite of Flower always grows in your own garden.*
> *The most beautiful Rainbow is seen from your porch.*
> *The Sun is strongest and the Moon is brightest from your window.*
> *Your Heart's desire is always present at your finger tips.*
> *When you seek out your wishes, they will find you.*
> *And when you open your heart to Life around you,*
> *You will always find that the best of Life is within you."*

And so it came to pass, armed with this advice, the young man moved resolutely forward to search out his destiny.

Upon hearing this, his mother miraculously recovered and began to shower him with love and attention. Instead of the bible, she brought out her I-Pod and resumed listening to her old favorites, Barbara Streisand, Elton John and John Lennon. The father, not to be undone, immediately perked up, and holding the latest photo of his son wearing a *"speedo"* outfit, he did not hesitate to brag to all, about his one and only. He even went so far as to admonish his sons-in-law to be more like him. *-Life was indeed getting good again.*

It did not take long to happen, nor was it a chance encounter. It was written in the ancient scrolls of life, that this union shall occur when the correct juxtaposition of events come to pass. *-And so it did, one warm and beautiful August day!*

On that fateful day he suddenly became aware of a strange feeling within him. He remembers it well. It was a hot, still summer's day, yet he felt a cool breeze blowing over him. There was not a sound to be heard, yet he was sure that he experienced the most beautiful music he had ever heard. He looked around to identify the source. There was no one of consequence. His sister, still smoking, his two nieces and a "friend", were busy in the kitchen, baking a Coconut Pie.

He had seen her many times before but never noticed her. But today something was different. He is still uncertain whether it was the smile, or her large black eyes, or the way she carried herself. Or maybe it was the confluence of all these things coming together in concert with destiny and the hands of fate. Whatever the reasons, the result was an almighty explosion of joy and contentment. It was indeed reminiscent of the description by Khalil Gibran of his first love, when,

"The heavens opened and his soul soared in joyous recognition of God's pleasure"

...... At long last, he knew he was in love! As you would expect, the reciprocation was instantaneous, and it is said, that Cupid collapsed with exhaustion from all the arrows that flew back and forth.

The word of this happening spread far and wide, and except for those homes where hopeful maidens had waited in silent anticipation, there was an explosion of joy and celebration. Her parents were justifiably happy, not only because of the boy and his family, but also because they had finally got rid of the last child and can now plan their "second honeymoon". His mother was no less overjoyed, for the girl possessed all the attributes to guarantee her being a good mother and wife. And his father is now something to behold, as he proudly struts and frets, cigarette in hand, feathers ruffled and voice booming;

"Heidi has nothing on me now!"

And tonight the story unfurls further as this momentous year closes. These children of destiny are beginning their journey along the true and tested path that many others have gone before. Their success or failure will depend not only on the love they feel for each other, but equally upon the depth of commitment and trust they are willing to offer upon the altar of marriage. For it is written:

> *"Much is expected, but for those who succeed,*
> *the rewards are indescribable."*

Also, let us not forget that they will always have the wisdom of *Papa Da* to guide them in times of concern, as they recall his words of assurance;

> *"He who loves all, deserves all".*
> *-The Butterfly Has Finally Landed!*

Life is Change

"The only thing constant in this world is Change"

 his quotation, taken from one of the songs by *India Arie,* the successful R and B singer, is to my mind one of the fundamental truths of life. Although this may sound paradoxical, Change defines life. Life cannot exist without change and in the absence of change there will be no life. It is Nature's most constant and most basic ingredient. Its existence ensures the continuity of life, and in many ways, is the yardstick by which all life is measured.

We see change occurring as an essential component in all the natural phenomena. They are present in the basic natural Environmental Cycles such as night and day, sunshine and rain, cold and warm, or in the Seasonal Variations occurring at predictable regular intervals of Spring, Summer, Autumn and Winter. They occur in every aspect of the Cycles of Life, beginning at the very moment of inception and continuing without interruption to the end. There can be no constancy in life, and by definition, life can only exist in a changing environment.

In similar manner, change is the most essential element in every aspect of human relationships. In all aspects of life, change serves to maintain and strengthen relationships and gives a reason for living. In our daily interactions our lives are sustained by the alternating periods of highs and lows we experience. Without these, we quickly stagnate and wither away. The healthiest and strongest relationships are invariably built on a foundation of constant and sometimes unpredictable, change. It is the glue that cements the relationship.

Change is constantly occurring, and its impact on each one of us is determined by the attitude we bring to bear. Many of us are content to passively submit to its influence, and like the floating leaf, be carried along life's journey like so much flotsam, ending in oblivion. But then there are others who are unwilling to accommodate to life's impositions and spend their time imposing their own will on their environment. By so doing, they succeed in modifying the natural changes or in creating new ones. These are the true pioneers, the dreamers, the innovators and the doers who ceaselessly contribute to the changing society. The over-riding hallmark of all these leaders is a willingness to stand against the forces of change and attempt to impose their personal will and direction.

From its very inception the history of the universe has been recorded and measured by the changes that have taken place. Its very birth was the result of certain cataclysmic changes scientists refer to as *"the Big Bang"*, resulting eventually in life itself. Since then there have been ongoing series of events occurring that have altered the conditions of survival resulting in a sequential evolution of species. This has continued unabated and include the cyclical changes, natural upheavals and catastrophes which when they occur produce changes locally and globally. It should be no surprise therefore to appreciate why Anthropologists spend their professional lives searching for the existence of changes in nature in order to explain its present development.

In every one of us, change is constantly occurring. Everything we do or say or think results in some type of change and conversely, change in anything will affect every one of us. Even at the microscopic level we are undergoing constant and unrelenting change. Whether it involves new growth or regeneration, organ function or degeneration, birth or death, change is the beginning and the end. The mere fact that we are here today is precisely because we were able to more readily adapt and change, while the less fortunate species disappeared because of reduced adaptability. The great Naturalist and Anthropologist *Sir Charles Darwin*, author of *"The Origin of Species"* stated this most eloquently in the following quotation:

> *"It is not the strongest of the species, or the most intelligent that survives. It is the one that is the most adaptable to change."*

Reinhold Niebuhr, the great American theologian and commentator, gave the following advice on the impact of change on our lives:

> *"Change is the essence of life.*
> *Be willing to surrender what you are, for what you could become."*

This statement is, in my opinion, the most potent advice that can be given to any one. The difference between success and failure is most often the result of our ability to deal with our changing environment. We admire those who have achieved success but fail to recognize that their achievement came only after they were able to accept the fundamental challenge of change. They were willing to take risks and venture into the unknown, while the others preferred to stay in their safe harbors and avoid the challenge of change.

Barack Obama, the 44th and current President of the United States of America, during his political campaign, was more direct and definitive in his comments when he spoke of the need for change:

> *"Change will not come if we wait for some other person or some other time. We are the ones we've been waiting for. -We are the Change that we seek."*

Many people have been critical of this statement as mere "political rhetoric" without an ounce of truth or validity. But whether this is true or not, does not take away the truly profound nature of the statement's content. Indeed, change to be truly effective, must begin with the individual and cannot wait for right time. Contrary to the general impression, change is never rigid but rather is very flexible and subject to great modification. It must never be your master, but always your servant. In fact meaningful change always begins with the individual and irrespective of the popular impression, is predominantly subjective and only rarely is it truly random.

Dr. Wayne Dyer, the internationally renowned American author and speaker, in one of his lectures in 2008, stated this fact in simple and dramatic terms:

"When you Change the way you look at things,
The things you look at, will Change."

-We will never lose sight of our desired state if we always remember to apply this rule to every thing we think or do.

Life and History

"History with its flickering lamp, stumbles along the trail of the past, trying to reconstruct its scenes, to revive its echoes, and kindle with pale gleams the passion of former days."

These eloquent words written by one of the world's elder statesmen and Nobel Prize Laureate, Sir Winston Churchill, exquisitely paints a true picture of the role of history in our lives, as we try to recount the events of the past and their impact on our future lives.

Life is really a continuum of events occurring in succession, leading from the past to the present and even into the future. All of human history is but a narrative description or record of these events not as they actually occurred, but rather as we have interpreted and assimilated them. As we travel along the road of life we learn and grow by the experiences of the moment and the lessons derived from them. Equally important to us is the knowledge of events of the past and our recall of them. Our historical perception is invariably subjective and as such our subsequent behavior is necessarily subjective. Conventional wisdom insists our concept of history is necessarily flawed and so too are our interpretation of events. Because of this we need to exercise caution in the use of history in our lives. James Baldwin, the famous black activist, was perhaps dramatic but still correct when he noted:

"People are trapped in history, and history is trapped in them."

Most historians will not hesitate to caution you to be careful how you use information derived from historical sources. Since they are merely records or interpretations of past events by people who may or may not have witnessed them, they are subject to the personal biases of the authors. Franklin P. Jones, the celebrated American humorist is credited with the following extremely insightful quotation:

> *"Perhaps nobody has changed the course of History*
> *as much as the historians"*

Any review of different accounts of the same historical event will quickly confirm this fact.

The same situation exists in our personal experiences. Too often we find ourselves in situations where we make life-changing decisions on the basis of an historical account, without questioning its validity or authenticity. We assume that because we know the source then that's good enough. I am sure that we can all think of examples of having come to conclusions based on certain accounts only to find out later that we were wrong, either because our information was biased, or our subjective interpretations were inaccurate. I certainly admit to many such examples in my own life.

The moral of this is that although we must rely on history to help us recall the past events affecting our lives and learn from them, we must however temper any conclusion arrived at with the knowledge that the information acquired is subject to bias and not necessarily strictly accurate. In this way we will avoid making decisions based on incorrect or inadequate information.

Whatever we do we should always keep in mind the famous quotation by *Aldous Huxley,* the outstanding English author and philosopher, publisher of the classic "The Brave New World":

> *"Man learns from History that Man does not learn from History."*

> *History is a set of lies agreed upon.*
> *.......Napoleon Bonaparte*

History is the sum total of the things that could have been avoided.
......Konrad Adenauer

Every true History must force us to remember that the past was once as
real as the present and as uncertain as the future.
......George Macaulay Trevelyan

History is the witness that testifies to the passing of time;
It illumines reality, vitalizes memory, provides guidance in daily life,
and brings us tidings of antiquity.
........Cicero

History is a kind of introduction to more interesting people than
we can possibly meet in our restricted lives; Let us not neglect the
opportunity.
........Dexter Perkins

History does not unfold: it piles up.
.........Robert M. Adams,

Even the most painstaking History is a bridge
across an eternal mystery.
........Bruce Catton,

There is nothing more dangerous than History used as a defense or
History used for preaching;
-History used as a tool is no longer history.
........Marcel Trudel

Living with Suicide

I'll show you a young man with so many reasons why;
There, but for fortune, go you or I.

.....JOAN BAEZ

A short while ago, like many others in the family, I received the horrific news that a young adolescent boy took his life in his parents' home during the early hours of the morning while everyone slept. Even I, with so many years of experience in care of medical and psychiatric problems, still find it difficult to accept such actions. The degree of trauma and pain suffered by the parents and the immediate family was, as to be expected, enormous and unbearable. The shock and loss experienced by his peers and associates, as judged by their reaction and their comments in the social media sites, was cataclysmic. Everyone searched for answers, and as happens in these situations, there was no shortage of answers. But all of them were merely the result of speculation and guessing. There was no definitive reason, and quite likely, there will never be any definitive reason for the tragedy. In the end a young man with so many reasons to live, was lost forever.

To God-fearing societies, Suicide is considered to be an abomination against God and except in the most extreme, radical societies, the action is considered to be illegal or taboo. Yet despite every effort to control it, each year over a million people in the world succeed in killing themselves. This statistic is even more frightening when you consider that for every successful attempt there are many more who have either attempted and failed, or seriously considered the possibility but for one of a number reasons never took any action. Sometimes

I wonder whether there is some truth in the statement made by a colleague of mine, supposedly in jest, during a discussion on the subject;

> *"We humans are all born with the instinct to take our lives at any time,*
> *and for any reason, and except for the grace of God and a little luck,*
> *we often do."*

Suicide is a worldwide scourge which, despite intensive attention, continues to increase at an alarming rate. The World Health Organization estimates that by the year 2020 there will be more than 1.5 million successful suicides and between 15 – 30 million unsuccessful attempts occurring annually. Each year it ranks in the top ten causes of death among adults and among the top three causes of death among adolescents. Further, although the records are not complete, the evidence points to the fact that the incidence of suicide in the Caribbean is surprisingly high and getting higher. This is a state of affairs that is unacceptable and demands the concerted efforts and understanding of everyone including parents, politicians, teachers and trained professionals as a matter of urgency.

Apart from the tragic consequences to the victim, Suicide is a very serious public health issue that has lasting, harmful effects on the family, the associates, and the community. Unfortunately these can persist for generations after. Unlike other events, this is further aggravated because of the unfortunate nature of the deed and the resulting ongoing "embarrassment". The action invariably leads to a sense of shame and withdrawal, and a genuine reluctance to seek appropriate help. When this is compounded with the inevitable feelings of responsibility and guilt experienced by the surviving family, the result is a further disintegration within the family structure leading to ongoing pain and suffering.

Suicide is a highly complex phenomenon, which despite extensive research, is still not clearly understood and unfortunately, not adequately managed. It is a behavioral action that involves poorly understood interactions between genetic, biochemical, psychological, societal, and cultural factors. Research shows that, especially in regard to adult victims, there are most often diagnosable underlying psychological conditions such as depressive illnesses, behavioral or personality disorders or substance abuse. This would suggest that, at least in regard to adult population, much more aggressive attention should be paid to the identification of early symptoms, the use of public education and the easy availability of competent resources including trained personnel, will have some effect on reducing the rising incidence of suicide.

Contrary to prevailing views, the problem of Adolescent Suicide is, in my view, somewhat different from Adult Suicide, and should be approached differently. Although depression is frequently mentioned as a risk factor in its causation and some sources suggest that this may as high as 75% of cases, I believe that the real causes are much more complex, and relate to the underlying demands of process of adolescence itself. At best, these years are an anxious and unsettling period for teenagers as they face the difficulties of transition into adulthood. It is the period in life where much is expected from them, but also one during which they undergo tumultuous changes physically, sexually and emotionally. They experience strong feelings of doubt, inadequacy, gender uncertainty and orientation and have deep seated fears of facing the future and expectations of adulthood, while they deal with the competitive demands of the present. It is a period that is often confusing and intimidating, causing some of them to feel isolated from family or authority, reluctant to seek guidance from them and unfortunately, turning to their peers for help. This is a formula for tragedy!

Compounding the situation is the very real social and environmental risk factors which we, as adults, do not understand and tend to take for granted. We assume that "they will learn as we did when we were their age" and make little or no effort to really understand our children. We tend to conveniently forget our own period of uncertainty and feelings of inadequacy which we experienced or witnessed in our time, and we try not to recall the names of our friends or contemporaries who fell by the wayside, or chose the ultimate solution because *"they could not take it anymore"*. I have no doubt that any one of us will have no difficulty to remember several examples among our own peers in our day.

It is this perceived apparent inadequacy or inability of parents and other people in authority to display the appropriate interest or worse, ignore the developing signs on the horizon, that in my mind give rise to some, if not all, the risk factors. As parents and adults, our expectations are directed to personal success and advancement for our children, and we give little attention to storm raging within and around them. To make matters worse, the current adolescent population has the added impact of the internet, and in particular such media sites as *Facebook*, to influence and further aggravate their conflicts. Not the least of which is the lingering fear of exposure, or ridicule or humiliation that, unlike previous generations, could occur and spread rapidly and lead to devastating consequences. Parents must recognize this very real possibility at all times and must take every opportunity to maintain open and ready flexibility, communication and willingness to understand their children.

Suicide among adolescents very rarely occurs on a planned, premeditated program. Rather it is much more an impulsive response to an unacceptable situation occurring in the individual's life. Whether that be a failed romance, bullying, criticism, sexual orientation or any of the many variations that has the potential of causing pain and embarrassment, especially when the victim feels unable to deal with it. I recall the response of a young girl after a failed attempt:

> *"I did it on a sudden decision, when I could not bear the thought that everybody will soon know about me. It seemed that this was the right thing to do especially since none of my family or friends really understood."*

Much has been written on this subject, but the following observation from the Social Science department of the University of Amsterdam, Holland, is impressive:

> *"Suicidal feelings should not be underestimated, they are real and powerful and immediate. The victims are driven by pain not choice. Suicide isn't chosen — it happens when pain exceeds the resources for coping with pain. But we do know that suicide is often a permanent solution to a temporary problem. And we also know that most people who once thought about killing themselves are now glad to be alive. They did not want to end their lives — they just wanted to stop the pain."*

Suicide is clearly a serious concern which is crying out for serious and concerted action from all of society. The only way we can hope to reduce the incidence of attempted and completed episodes in our community is by establishing comprehensive programs involving all members of society. In situations where meaningful efforts in education, sensitization and improved communications among all groups have occurred there has been significant improvement both in the reduction of events and in the general welfare of our teenage population. But if we hope to be successful we must include everyone involved in the care and concern of our adolescents;

-<u>Health authorities</u> must provide adequate professional support such as Social and Psychological personnel to deal with the very real adolescent problems of adjustment and orientation and to identify and correct the symptoms of depression so common at that age. We cannot allow the present pattern of leaving them to their own resources and not expect increasing disasters.

-<u>Families</u> must be educated to their responsibility in the welfare of their children. Negative family functioning is undoubtedly a strong risk factor. There is a very strong association of suicidal and other emotional ideation among teenagers with a family history of suicide, substance abuse, marital conflict, physical violence and marital conflict including divorce, neglect or abandonment. Studies suggest that family conflicts precipitate at least 20% of completed suicides and 50% of attempted. Successful family interactions result in providing the necessary protective factor, secure safety net and open communications that are needed to help overcome any challenge or conflict.

-<u>School personnel</u> play an equally vital role in the lives of their students. The ongoing contact in the classroom and in the hallways may provide an opportunity for early identification and effective prevention of potential behavior. Any change in academic performance or behavior or emotional response may herald an early sign of trouble. This is even more important since students are more willing to confide in their teacher than their parents. But for this to take place, teachers must make the effort, be alert and proactive in the school.

In the end, the only chance we have to try to curb this scourge in society, and to protect our children from impulsively destroying their sacred, God-given life lies in our willingness, as parents, teachers, professionals or support personnel to recognize our individual and group responsibilities and to take steps to familiarize ourselves with appropriate knowledge. Normal, healthy adolescent development occurs in the context of a loving, secure, mutually respectful setting where there are responsible and mature relationships. Until they are comfortable to express their concerns, positive or negative, to parents and teachers and not be afraid of ridicule or embarrassment they are likely to keep them to themselves or worse, seek out the advice of their peers.

This is the challenge we face as we continue to witness the senseless loss and destruction of our children.

No one ever lacks a good reason for suicide.
......Cesare Pavese

Suicide is not a remedy.
.....James A. Garfield

Suicide is the remedy of pain
.....Matt Hartman

More than one soul dies in a suicide
.....Author Unknown

When people kill themselves, they think they're ending the pain, but all they're doing is passing it on to those they leave behind
......*Jeannette Walls*

Sometimes I wonder if Suicides aren't in fact sad guardians of the meaning of life
.....*Vaclav Havel*

Stories of Conversion, Transformation and Acceptance

"I am Jesus," the Lord answered. "I am the one you are so cruel to. Now get up and go into the city, where you will be told what to do."

The above description of St. Paul's conversion is taken from *The Acts of the Apostles, chapter 9:1-19*. It records how Saul (or Paul) of Tarsus, formerly a ruthless enemy and a relentless persecutor of the early Christian Church, was converted by God's grace to become one of its main supporters and spokesman. His transformation was as dramatic as it was overwhelming, and his change from one who killed Christians to one who was eventually killed because of his beliefs in Jesus Christ. It is often used as a paramount example of the place of Conversion as the heart of Christian experience.

In one way or another, examples of this kind of experience are exceedingly common in our day-to-day living, and I have no doubt that anyone of us will have no difficulty in recalling multiple encounters in ourselves and in others, when we witnessed a change that was entirely unexpected. The world's books are similarly filled with stories of people who, as a result of a conversion, have changed the course of history. In all the instances, these occurrences generally follow a distinct, easily identifiable pathway which first involves an event or series of events taking place causing an awareness or insight to develop and leading to a *conversion* and a change in attitude and perception. This is then followed by a period of assimilation leading ultimately to *transformation* and finally to *acceptance* or internalization. From then on the conversion is complete and a commitment to the new view is established.

Conversions are most commonly seen and reported in relation to religious events when as a result of a personal experience the individual undergoes a transformation leading to a new acceptance of the teaching and the principles of the religion. Over the centuries since the coming of Jesus Christ, the stories of conversion to Christianity by individuals, families, groups and even countries are well documented and easily accessible. There have been thousands of instances of people who have given up their previous lives to follow the ways of the particular religion. They have all contributed to the improvement of the people and the environment they shared and we have all come to accept the wisdom of their decisions. All of these people have earned the respect and admiration of succeeding generations for the sacrifices they made, as much as the good they achieved. They are held in the highest regards by all.

So too are the great humanitarian leaders who have appeared over the years. People like Mahatma Gandhi, Martin Luther King, Jr. and Nelson Mandela whose conversion to their cause of peace among people have resulted in profound changes occurring across the world. A study of the lives of any of these people will invariably show that in all the cases they did not arrive at their final position by a process of slow evolution, but rather as a result of the existing circumstances and their subsequent conversation, transformation and subsequent acceptance of their special role.

But there is also a group of people who, as a result of their special response to a catastrophic event, have and will continue to earn them the greatest respect from all of their peers. We can all relate to them, they live among us and are a source of profound respect and admiration from us, if only because we recognize that their action is above anything we can achieve. They don't ask for special recognition, nor do they believe that they are extraordinary people. They believe that they are doing what they were meant to do under the special circumstances in which they find themselves.

In my career over many years, I have had the opportunity to meet or to learn about a good number of these people. In every instant, when I encountered these individuals, I am overwhelmed with respect and admiration for what has been achieved and above all, by the faith and strength of character displayed. Consider the following examples;

-A 67 year man who was previously in good health. He was a dynamic businessman who had achieved great success in his private and professional life, and who enjoyed all the good things that this offered. As a result of a freak accident and medical mismanagement he sustained a broken neck leading to almost complete paralysis below the neck. After an early disappointment he quickly settled down and became quite positive announcing that God has given him the opportunity to use his illness to help others. He remained positive for as long as he lived. He had indeed experienced a conversion, undergone a transformation and achieved genuine acceptance.

-Nicholas James Vujicic, an Australian of Croatian descent was born with a rare condition, *Tetramelia Disorder*, characterized by almost complete absence of his upper and lower limbs. After an early life filled with anger and resentment including suicidal considerations, he became a very successful and much sought after Christian motivational speaker. He credits the change to a newspaper article he read when he was about 13 years old, about a disabled man who had managed to achieve great things and help many people. He realized that this was an opportunity to use his skills to serve God and his conversion was complete.

-A 68 year old man ravaged with end stage cancer, who had spent the last few months exhibiting intense frustration and anger as only a person in his final days without hope or acceptance, can feel. It became so difficult that even the professional caregivers found their job seriously compromised. One morning he awoke a changed man, more accepting and more tolerant. He continued to maintain this demeanor to the very end and as a result, his family was gratefully able to spend this last period building meaningful and rewarding memories. To the end, he was sure that he was visited by an apparition, whom he is convinced was Jesus Christ, and was given certain reassurances. That indeed was the seed of his conversion, the reason for his transformation and the basis of his unwavering acceptance.

These are but three of many examples of this phenomenon at work. Like many others I see this as a blessing, while others will argue that these are merely examples of denial developed to shield the individual from further pain and suffering. But the sense of peace and equanimity these people radiate as they go about their tasks speaks loudly of their acceptance. It affords them and all those associated with them the opportunity to come to terms with the situation and to make the most of the time allotted. Regret is replaced with hope and anger replaced with patience and understanding. All of which argues against this being more than chance or coincidence and for the direct involvement of a power beyond our control. Perhaps this is what St. Paul meant when he wrote in his *letter to the Ephesians, chapter 4:22-24:*

> *"You should put away the old self of your former way of life, corrupted through deceitful desires, and be renewed in the spirit of your minds, and put on the new self created in God's way in the righteousness and holiness of truth."*

Living with Violence

"America is, by far, the most violent country in the world when measured against comparable, industrialized nations. Violence is deeply rooted in our society and has become woven into the fabric of the American lifestyle. A culture of violence has emerged that invades our lives at every level, from our most intimate relationships at home to our schools and work environments.

This statement contained in the 2007-2008 Annual Report by Edmund R. Brown, Jr. California's Attorneys General, accurately crystallizes the true status of violence in America. Compared with the other advanced countries, America has the highest rate of prison incarcerations, with more than 2 million prisoners at any time, a number that equates to more than quarter of the world's prison population. The country has consistently reported the highest homicide rates in the industrialized world and even more frightening, more people possess some form of weapon for self-protection than all the rest of the world's population put together.

The increasing aura of violence in our society and our awareness of violence around us has changed the way we live in our cities. In more and more areas of our cities, because of the increase in gang formation and drug violence, drive-by shootings, daylight muggings and indiscriminate attacks we are beginning to feel like prisoners in our homes and neighborhoods, afraid to venture out alone. It should come as no surprise therefore that some of the fastest growing industries in this country are private security and weapons.

Although we publicly lament the existence of violence in our cities, in our society and in our schools, we also are guilty of sending mixed messages to our children. By encouraging wanton violence on our TV screens and in our cinemas, by highlighting and encouraging violence in sport and entertainment, on the playing field and in the video games, by making and endorsing heroes of crooks and criminals, we succeed in indoctrinating our children that violence in society is acceptable, and worse, by our silence, we encourage them to think that violence is a reasonable alternative.

Even our media, by their eagerness and insistence in reporting all the gory details of violent incidents, contribute to the glorification of violence as a means of achieving solution. By their endless reporting of incidents, repeated over and over, they succeed in persuading people that such behavior is normal and acceptable, making the next action easier to contemplate. Very rarely is an effort made to register the public abhorrence of the behavior and the genuine resentment of the perpetrators. Society, while recognizing that the perpetrator needs help, must not lose sight of it's responsibility to punish the action, protect the victims and above all, to take the necessary steps to correct the underlying causes. The recent outbreak of violence between the police and some black communities is no different both in the outcome or management. Clearly we can not begin to deal with the problems until some consistent, rational attitudes are adopted.

Tragically we, as individuals and as a society, have yet to learn the lessons from the actions around us. We continue to witness horrific examples of grossly abnormal behavior among our young people such as the Columbine school massacre, the vicious and brutal attack on the homeless and the gang-like act of publicly setting a boy on fire. Though occurring in different areas and under different circumstances, these and the thousands of others taking place daily, appear to have one constant denominator, the progressive disintegration of society's standards and responsibilities.

But violence is not a disease that can be passed on from person to person and cannot be treated by simply administering a local remedy. Violence is a reflection of the society and represents the worse aspect of the prevailing attitudes within the society. As I see it, even in the midst of so much advancement in the quality and opportunity in our lives, our society has become too indifferent, too immune to its responsibility towards maintaining the quality and consistency needed to ensure the right standards. We cannot expect our children to do otherwise when we ourselves abandon our own principles, by continuing to glorify violence, by ignoring the needs of our children, by abandoning our family responsibilities as we spend more time away from the home. When we add to this the scourge of easy accessibility of drugs, reduced controls in the schools, increasing domestic violence and marital breakdowns, and so many other social problems, one should not be surprised of the present epidemic of violence.

And yet the answers to preventing this escalation of violence can be simple and effective if we take the time to recognize the causes and make the effort to correct them. As a society, we need to reconsider how we glorify violence in all its forms, most especially in the fields of entertainment, sports and video games. Equally we must take time to provide quality time to our children, to encourage them away from the present exposure to the many negative contacts and to provide positive opportunities for growth. To achieve this we need to change drastically from the present direction, something we loathe to do. We have yet to learn that the real truth of the statement made by the noted American author, *Mary McCarthy*:

"In violence we forget who we are"

Violence shapes and obsesses our society,
and if we do not stop being violent we have no future.
....Edward Bond

"Games don't create violence,
They reflect the violent society we already live in."
..... annonymous

The violence in society, I'm afraid, is perpetrated
by the people at the top.
.....Rob Walton

"If it's natural to kill, how come men have to go into
training to learn how?"
...Joan Baez

"We do not need guns and bombs to bring peace,
we need love and compassion."
.....Mother Teresa

Collective fear stimulates herd instinct,
and tends to produce ferocity toward those
who are not regarded as members of the herd."
.....Bertrand Russell

"Violence is as American as cherry pie"
.....H. R. Schiffman

Life Closing

Every road will eventually end. The astute traveler takes cognizance of this fact and plans accordingly.

By preparing adequately, the journey becomes a trip that can be turned to one of peaceful and joyful anticipation.

But alas, this is not always so and as a result many a traveler will find themselves in anxious disappointment. The journey becomes a nightmare to all concerned.

Rather than happy memories, the end of the journey brings nothing but pain, suffering and regrets.

On Growing Old

*M*any years ago, one of France's greatest personalities, a talented actor, comedian and goodwill ambassador, *Maurice Chevalier,* commented, to the delight of his sold out audience that:

"Old age isn't so bad, when you consider the alternatives."

He continued to lead a full and active life until he retired in 1968 at age 80 years, 4 years before he died. His statement however has continued on, taking a life of its own and has been used globally as an excellent comment on getting old.

For most people, particularly those who have led a full and active life, the thought of growing old with all its perceived handicaps and inadequacies, can be daunting and humbling. Very few people ever admit to looking forward to old age, and when they do, there is always a slight hint of nostalgia and disappointment in their voices. But the reality is that irrespective of what we do, or try to do, or hope for, the nature of events are such that life leads relentlessly and inexorably to an end and the best we can do under the circumstances, is to try to do what we can to "enjoy the ride." The fact is, despite all the claims made and all the hopes we harbor, there is only one alternative to getting old and irrespective of who you are or what you do, it is only a matter of time before each one of us arrive at that final point.

During the early phases of our lives few of us ever give any thought to the aspect of growing old. We become so deeply involved in building relationships, establishing careers and finding out more about ourselves that we make no plans beyond the present. As we spend every minute of each day in dealing with the needs and the demands of that day, we are not concerned, nor do we have the time or the inclination to be concerned, with planning for the future. It does not take much to persuade ourselves that there will be time to think about getting old later, but for now this is not relevant in today's needs. And even as we encounter and deal with older people along the way, we seldom pause enough to think about ourselves eventually joining their ranks. Instead we use these encounters to improve ourselves by learning from them, or competing with them or even replacing them. This after all is the way of life.

Someone once described life as being a journey climbing up a mountain. You start at the bottom slowly and deliberately as you learn the art of climbing. As you progress upwards, you gain assurance and travel further and plan more confidently. You are satisfied as you survey what you have achieved, and you are encouraged to make plans for your continued progress. Your journey is exciting and rewarding and you cannot wait to reach the top. However, as you get to the top, you soon find that this euphoria does not last and the journey gets more difficult, there are more obstacles and you realize that the road was getting tougher and that you are not coping as well, as you arrive at the top. Then you begin to descend downhill. The journey going down seems to be much faster and you begin to get the feeling that it takes a lot more effort to achieve than you previously needed to expend. You realize, ready or not, old age is catching up and sooner or later the road will reach an end. You do what you can to slow the decline, you might even succeed temporarily but in the end you cannot hold back the inevitable.

But old age does not have to be the frightening monster that it is portrayed to be. You do not have to feel like an old garment to be tossed aside as the impetuous youth take over. Nor should it be the opposite where we feel committed, at all cost and with increasing effort, to hold on to the present, completely oblivious of the problems we cause or the damage we do. These actions are both inappropriate and even worse, can and do result in unnecessary pain, frustration and unhappy experiences.

In fact, old age, properly managed, can be the best and most satisfying phase of living. Older people, having lived through and coped with a bewildering series of experiences, are better able to solve problems, to control their emotions, to accept misfortune and admit responsibility. The advancing years have generally made them more tolerant, less prone to anger or to pass judgment, and more willing to understand and to forgive. And even as their health becomes increasingly compromised, they become much more accepting and therefore more cheerful. This, to my mind, is the single most gratifying finding in individuals who have successfully adapted to the demands of getting old and if handled correctly is indeed one of life's greatest empowerments.

Every person is endowed with their own peculiar personality, attitude, ambition, image and expectation which impact upon their individual lives in their own unique way. It is not surprising therefore that they each approach old age in their own special way. While a small percentage will inevitably reject the obvious and continue on as if there is no end, the great majority will, at some point along the way, take time to look back and review their lives and their work. If you live long enough and live right enough, your joy and satisfaction will more than compensate your own fading star. This indeed is the true reality of life!

As I look back upon my own journey along life's road and recall my experiences as I crossed over from one stage to another and remember the many mistakes I made and equally, the many correct decisions I took, I am left with a sense of contentment. In a paradoxical way, getting old does have its advantages for it implies that you have lived long enough to have done things worth doing, to have influenced people who appreciate your efforts, to have memories worth treasuring. In a small way you hope to have made your world a little better than you found it. *Henry Wadsworth Longfellow,* the great American author, poet and educator spoke on behalf all those older people when he wrote:

> *"For age is an opportunity no less*
> *Than youth itself, though in another dress,*
> *And as the evening twilight fades away,*
> *The sky is filled with stars invisible by day."*

Grow old along with me! The best is yet to be.
The last of life, For which the first was made.
- - - - Robert Browning

A man is not old until regrets take the place of dreams.
........John Barrymore

There are none are so old as those who have outlived enthusiasm.
.......Henry David Thoreau

To know how to grow old is the master-work of wisdom, and one of the most difficult chapters in the great book of living.
.......Henri Amiel

We've put more effort into helping folks reach old age than into help-ing them enjoy it.
........Frank A. Clark

The tragedy of old age is not that one is old but that one is young.
......Oscar Wilde

Age is a prison from which we cannot escape.
.......Morrow Bourne

Like our shadows, our wishes lengthen as our sun declines.
........Edward Young

Inside every older person is a younger person wondering what happened.
........Jennifer Yane

If youth but know, and old age only could.
......Henri Estienne

Youth is a blunder, Manhood, a struggle Old age, a regret.
............Benjamin Disraeli,

Nobody grows old merely by living a number of years.
We grow old by deserting out ideals. Years may wrinkle the skin,
But to give up enthusiasm wrinkles the soul.
.... Samuel Ullman

Looking into the Eyes of Alzheimer's

"Alzheimer's disease however, robs the person not only of the present and the future, but also of the past, as all memory of prior events, relationships and people slips away."

These words, were recorded by *Professor Stephen Sapp of the University of Miami, Florida,* in an article entitled, *"Living with Alzheimer's."* They describe precisely and accurately the disease scourge that is Alzheimer's. Originally identified by the German Psychiatrist, *Dr. Alois Alzheimer,* it is the most common form of a group of disorders called *Dementia* which has no cure. They cause progressive deterioration of mind and body and are invariably fatal. Ultimately, death results from external factors such as pneumonia, septicemia or organ failure.

Dementia is a disease that robs a person not only of their memories, their intelligence, their reason and their personality, but also of the most important component of their existence, their human dignity. As the disease progresses, the patients are engulfed by a complex and confusing dilemma where simple tasks give rise to monumental concerns. This occurs at the stage when there is just enough insight that something is just not right and can cause significant distress. As it progresses, the disease gives rise to altered perception and interpretation leading to unreasonable actions and behaviors. This is made worse by the public's inability to understand the behavior and the tendency to become increasingly critical and antagonistic. The consequences of this situation result only in aggravating an already difficult and regrettable state all around.

As a physician with more than fifty years of active practice, I have seen and dealt with a good share of patients in various degrees of Alzheimer's and, as would be expected, have had to deal with its effect on the patient as well as on members of the immediate family. Yet it would be fair to say that, despite all these years of direct experience I, like all my medical colleagues, recognize how much more we need to know about this disease. Although we are able to recognize and demonstrate the profound changes in the appearance of the individual's brain as it progresses to the advanced stages, there is still a great diversity of opinion among experts as to how much of someone's understanding and recognition remains as the disease continues on its relentless path to oblivion. The real truth is that, despite extensive, on-going research by centers all over the world, we are still a very long way from understanding, far less reversing, this disease process.

Society in general has developed a very ambivalent approach to coping with this increasing problem and in fact prefers to ignore its existence as much as it can. The majority of physicians, aware of the complex, time-consuming and unrewarding nature of the disease, prefer to avoid commitment as far as possible, and at best, provide episodic care as needed. Family members and caregivers, in the absence of adequate guidance on this subject and intimidated by the confusing presentation, are often left to their own resources to provide appropriate care and to avoid doing anything to aggravate the situation. This unfortunate situation is further compounded by the increasing fragmentation of the extended family and the economic demands on the individual members, which serve to restrict opportunity to do more. The result is that Alzheimer's disease, quite unlike any other disease complex, is notorious for the very wide range of care provided to the unfortunate victims. This range spreads the full continuum from the very best care possible, to the very worst and at times, to inhumane neglect. Further, unlike most other medical disorders, the situation is not necessarily improved with increasing socio-economic status.

Everyone who has been in a position to observe victims of this disease will attest to the fact that even in the advanced stages when the patient is rendered increasingly helpless, mute and uncommunicative, there are periods, sometimes brief and short-lived, when they appear to recognize and to understand and to show appropriate responses. I, like the great majority of my colleagues, am convinced that these islands of clarity, these moments of awareness when the patient is able to escape the walls of their prison for a fleeting second and join the world of reality is evidence that all is not lost. Yet despite all the apparent advances so far achieved, we are still very far from truly understanding the working of the brains of people suffering from Dementia. Therefore in the absence of any meaningful advances it is difficult and premature to use the label "permanent" or "irreversible." Clearly there is urgent need to understand and to educate society in all the aspects of this profound mind-destroying disease. Equally, it should serve to negate the argument, becoming increasingly popular and widely supported by politicians and civic leaders, to justify the statement that we are *"wasting valuable resources and personnel in such hopeless endeavors."*

Yet as you speak to relatives and caregivers who spend many hours in caring and sharing their lives with the defenseless victims of this vicious disease, you occasionally encounter certain times and occasions when you are overwhelmed by the aura of peace and love that radiates. These occasions come as a breath of fresh air to the physician and serve to reinforce his confidence in the essential goodness in mankind. I myself will always remember a young woman, Kim, who has chosen to devote her life to providing as much comfort and support as she possibly can to counteract the vicious, destructive consequences of this cursed disease. The peaceful acceptance and the joyful optimism she brings with everything she does is indeed a blessing of love, and a lesson to us all. In a very small but meaningful way, I see these acts as true and genuine manifestations of the love which Christ spoke about to his disciples and expressed so selflessly by such great people as St. Francis of Assisi, Blessed Teresa of Kolkata and Albert Schweitzer, and by so many others who quietly serve in this thankless setting.

In my own personal life, these last few years have been spent in the difficult and unfortunate circumstances of having to witness the steady and progressive decline of someone who meant a great deal to me. I witnessed the relentless, progressive disintegration of a beautiful and vibrant personality as it descended into the hell of oblivion. But I also saw the single-minded dedication and the blazing love that emanated from the eyes of the children and the caregivers and the profound peace and love that pervaded the whole environment, and I am humbled by their devotion. Unfortunately, and very tragically, this is by no means the prevailing attitude and behavior available to the great majority of patients, who by and large, have to spend their waning years lost in a cloud of apathy.

There is still a great need and an urgency to educate and inform society in general, on the fundamental needs and expectation for the disease. To this end, the *National Institute on Aging* in 2000 published an excellently written and informative booklet entitled *Caring for a Person with Alzheimer's Disease*. I strongly endorse this as required reading by everyone. In addition, the local and national *Alzheimer's Associations* provide a good deal of information and support to family and caregivers at a local level. Unfortunately their services and advice is not being sought as often as they should.

Against all this unfortunate and painful suffering, I am left with great disappointment and an unyielding indictment against a society such as ours that is much more concerned with glorifying young athletes with absurd and obscene remunerations, and of entertainers who accumulate large amounts of wealth and reward us with their bizarre immoral and sexual encounters. Yet we find it difficult to provide the necessary education, support and resources to help our less fortunate brothers and sisters to navigate through the raging fires of one of the worst and most soul destroying disease.

In the end, the tragedy of Alzheimer's disease is as much a reflection of our personal and societal responsibility as it is a matter of medical management. In this context, both as a physician and as an involved member of society, I cannot possibly do any better than to remind the reader of a quotation of *Blessed Teresa of Kolkata* whose words are as profound as they are touching and relevant:

> *"Speak tenderly to them. Let there be kindness in your face,*
> *in your eyes, in your smile, in the warmth of your greeting.*
> *Always have a cheerful smile. Don't only give your care,*
> *But give your heart as well".*

Losing a Child

"There's no tragedy in life like the death of a child.
Things never get back to the way they were."

The great Army General, Elder Statesman and former President, General Dwight D. Eisenhower expressed these sentiments after the death of his own three year old son in 1921, from which he never ever fully recovered. I cannot think of any experience more traumatic or more devastating than the unexpected loss of a child. Not only is the immediate pain and grief unbearable, but it never goes away even with the passage of time. It is considered by most experts as the leading cause of prolonged and unremitting grief that causes profound changes in the lives of the parents and the immediate family.

The fact is there are very few families that have been spared the trauma of having to deal with such an occurrence at least once in its lifetime. More often the family is confronted with several such events involving children at different ages occurring at different times. Each one of these gives rise to equally intense and different reactions as they contribute to the progressive distortion in thinking and in behavior among the survivors. In many instances this eventually leads to a series of conflicting behavioral responses that can result in the ultimate disintegration of the family.

The effects are invariably complex and produce widely varying manifestations that could range from aggressive uncontrollable behavior to complete fear and withdrawal. The parents develop intense feelings of grief and loss that are accompanied with guilt and regret. They experience a multitude of bizarre physical and emotional symptoms. They become restless, volatile and unpredictable. They develop a bewildering combination of symptoms which renders them effectively non-functional. Their normal patterns of eating, sleeping and activity are turned upside down. They tend to question themselves and others involved, searching for answers. These feeling never completely abate, even with the passage of time and they are never the same persons after.

The siblings also, are at risk of developing a variety of reactions that could include feelings of guilt, anger and regression. They develop feelings that they may be next and respond often in confusing and paradoxical ways. Denial is most often manifested in such unconventional ways that it is difficult to predict the outcome. They often lose the fear of death or vulnerability to illness and begin to act in ways that can result in personal injury. Problems in behavior, increased antisocial activity and deteriorating performance are not uncommon. The younger children are often confused about the impact of death and find it difficult to accept its permanence. Mourning is very difficult and often accompanied with profound regressive symptoms of fear, vulnerability and dependence.

In my own practice, I am so conscious of the short and long term effects that occur following the loss of a child and the lasting impact on the physical and emotional states that I often include it in my deliberations and management plans. Too often have I been fooled in ascribing reasons for behavior until I include this factor in my diagnosis. Anything that is remotely related to the child's demise is likely to create intense feelings and resistances. Hence the increased reluctance or lack of eagerness exhibited to seek the help of the physician in the hope that this will not happen again. In this respect, it is of vital importance that all concerned with the care and support of the family recognize the risks and the possibility and to act in their best interest. I have often referred to that wonderful, sensitive quotation by Professor John DeFrain of the Department of Family Studies in the University of Nebraska which says it all:

> *"The death of a child is like a stone cast into the stillness of a quiet pool; the concentric ripples of despair sweep out in all directions, affecting many, many people."*

Grief fills the room up of my absent child,
Lies in his bed, walks up and down with me,
Puts on his pretty look, repeats his words,
Remembers me of his gracious parts,
Stuffs out his vacant garments with his form.
William Shakespeare

There is no footprint too small to leave an imprint on this world.
Author unknown

Grieving the loss of a child begins the day the child passes;
And ends the day the parent joins them.
Author unknown

Living with Death and Dying

An Overview

"Everybody is born with an expiry date."

This statement was made to me many years ago by a friend, now deceased, after he was diagnosed with cancer of the Lung. It has forever impressed me by its profound simplicity and truth. In just a few simple words he easily confirmed a fact that appears to be increasingly questioned and challenged by the modern world.

Since the beginning of time, the status of death and dying has held a dominant position in man's thinking. In primitive societies, where religion and culture were closely inter-related, death was tied to life in a cyclical way. Death, like the seasonal and agricultural cycles, was necessary in order to lead to rebirth or resurrection in one form or another. Primitive rituals reflected this belief universally. People accepted the inevitability of death as part of the cycle of human life. The Native Americans for example, view life and death as parts of a circular movement, wherein the process merely represents a transformation and not finality, and after death the spirit continues to live on. Buddhists always celebrate death. For even though dying means losing someone close in this world, they believe that only through death, can they be one step closer to *Nirvana,* the perfect state of mind.

In Western cultures, the attitudes of the society have a huge impact on people's perception of death. So also are the influences of the various religious groups, which affect and determine people's attitudes. Fear of the unknown has always been one of the most common factors affecting our approach towards death, giving rise to profound anxiety. However, Christians are taught to view death as not to be denied or feared, but as something precious and even welcomed for the blessings it brings with the promise of eternal life hereafter.

Unlike previous generations, with the increasing impact of the medical and scientific advances in diagnosis and treatment, the attitude towards death is being greatly modified. The modern world seems to be losing the sense of death as being an inevitable consequence of living. More and more, death is being regarded as something that should not happen, and should not be allowed to happen. As a result we find ourselves demanding and expecting everything be done, at all cost, to keep life going, without regard to the resulting quality or certainty of the life. In some ways these days, death is regarded as taboo and it is considered impolite to speak of its reality and its inevitability.

This confusion is compounded by the increasing trend towards the widespread exposure of death in the media to children at a very early age. It has the effect of removing the aura of the unknown, and gives rise to the development of a variety of conflicting attitudes towards life and death, leading to confusing and unrealistic interpretations and expectations. The result is an increasing difficulty of acceptance and ability to accommodate.

Whatever the situation, we should recognize that there can be no standardization of attitude to death. Each person has his or her own view of death and its consequences. Although much of this is based on the prevailing society's attitudes and beliefs, each one has to deal with the loss in one's own way. Clearly a sudden unexpected loss or the death of a younger person carries a greater impact than an older or terminally ill person. Children are generally much more accepting because they do not understand the meaning of finality and expect the loss to be corrected in some way. But in the end, there is no easy position except the fact is that death is as certain and as inevitable as any other cycle of nature.

For my own self, as a practicing Physician for more than 50 years, I have encountered and dealt with a wide range of attitudes, responses and reactions to the anticipation and reality of death of my patients and their families. I still find it difficult to predict or influence other people's attitudes. To me death is merely a stop on the journey of life. What matters more is the quality of life you lead. For I firmly believe that a person who has lived a full and fulfilling life has no reason to fear death. There is a purpose in dying. It is but a stop on the continuum of life as I have stated previously in describing my concept of "life" as contained in the following statement:

> "To me, life is not a random series of transient, overlapping, unrelated experiences, destined to be consigned to oblivion upon completion. I believe instead, life is a precious expression of a greater plan in which our time spent on earth is but a short segment of a journey which began in eternity and will continue to eternity".

I believe that part of our living must of necessity involve our preparation for dying. In our early years, we were consumed with life, vitality and achieving our dreams, so death occupied a very minor portion in our thinking. But as we grew older we are faced increasingly with the natural urge to consider the likelihood of dying and spend time in making preparation. I am always bothered by those who avoid or are afraid to deal with the subject or spend all their time and effort trying to "beat it". By doing this, you end up cheating yourself of the reality and the opportunity of peaceful acceptance. Rather like the analogy of the *"half-full/half-empty glass"*. The person who thinks of his life as half-empty is destined to spend all his days in constant search without fulfillment, even to the end. While the other who views his life as half-full will continue to enjoy his life as he consumes the rest to the end.

In this context, I am reminded of that beautiful letter written by the *Rev. Henry Scott Holland*, the 19th century English clergyman, in regard to his own impending death, and sent to all his friends and family after he died, under the caption, *"All is Well"*:

> "To my beloved family and friends,
>   Death is nothing at all. I've only slipped away into the next room. I am I, and you are you. Whatever we were to each other then, that we are still. Call me by my old familiar names. Speak to me in the same

easy way which you always used to. Put no difference in your tone. Wear no air of solemnity or sorrow. Laugh as we always laugh at the little jokes we enjoyed together. Play, smile, think of me, Pray for me, let my name ever be the household name it ever was. Let it be spoken without effect, without a ghost of a shadow on it. Life means all that it ever was. There is absolutely unbroken continuity. Why should I be out of mind because I am out of sight? I am but waiting for you an interval, somewhere very close, just around the corner. …...All is well!"

The Final Journey

"There is a dignity in dying that doctors should not dare to deny. For death begins with Life's first breath"

The above statement by an unknown author has always impressed me for its profound simplicity and dramatic accuracy, and deserves much more than passing notice. Like the clergyman, the physician is expected to play a pivotal role in the life of the dying patient and the family, especially during the period of "the final journey" and beyond. Unfortunately this does not often happen because doctors are very rarely trained to recognize and deal with end-of-life issues. Dr. Ira Byock in his excellently written book, *"Dying Well"*, summarized this in the following manner:

"The medical profession most commonly approaches dying as if it were solely a problematic medical event. From the first day in medical school, doctors are taught to approach patients by defining a set of medical problems to be solved. People come to doctors with "problems". For each case a problem list must be developed through which both physical and psycho-social problems can be addressed".

Dealing with dying is much more than just a consideration of the etiology of a collection of symptoms and signs, diagnosing the problem and providing a treatment plan. This is what physicians are trained to do and are generally confident in executing. Rather, it is a very personal experience that requires a very special and individual approach tailored to meet the needs of the patient and the family. The physician is uniquely placed to facilitate and ease the pain and uncertainty of the situation. By being available to answer questions, being honest and caring and above all, being especially sensitive to the fears and the anxieties of all concerned, he will go a long way in assisting everyone to cope with this daunting and terrifying period.

In my own personal experience, after actively practicing medicine for more than half a century, no aspect of my practice has given me as much satisfaction as the occasions when I was able to successfully help my patient and the family cross over in peace, faith, dignity and acceptance. Because of my Psychiatric background, I was perhaps better equipped to understand, recognize and possibly identify cues from the patient and to deal with them. But I believe I was able to achieve greater success when I learned to accommodate the strict objective, scientific training I received in medical school with a personal subjective, faith-based viewing of life and death as a continuum, controlled by the hand of the Almighty.

As I have stated previously, I believe life is a precious expression of a greater plan in which our time spent on earth is but a short segment of a journey which began in eternity and will continue to eternity. Because of this, I see the process of dying, not as the end of the journey, but merely a stage along the path, and as such I view my role as a physician as doing my best to facilitate the change. *Sri Chinmoy Kumar Ghose*, the great Indian spiritual teacher and philosopher who recently died, described this concept exquisitely in the following quotation:

> *"Death is not the end. Death can never be the end.*
> *Death is the road. Life is the traveler.*
> *The Soul is the Guide."*

As I see it, the approach to dealing with death and the dying patient is essentially eclectic, encompassing a variety of approaches from many sources including the attitude and expectations of the patient and family, the immediate and long-term prognosis, society's mores and the extent of religious and social support available. The physician's role is crucial, not only in providing honest and accurate information concerning the prognosis and treatment options, but equally important, in assessing the real need of the individual and providing personal understanding and strength, without resorting to denial or lying. He must be available to prepare and guide his patient through the difficult passage, to ease the pain and above all, to offer hope and reassurance.

It is generally assumed that patients would prefer not to hear the real truth, but rather be given hope of recovery even when the situation is hopeless. This is a mistake, for by encouraging this we rob the patient and the family of the opportunity of coming to terms without lingering regrets. I prefer to choose the approach of Rev. Forrest Church who before he died in 2006 wrote:

> *"Many people who are dying have an opportunity but sometimes don't have the imagination to seize it. And that is, to turn my life into a prayer, to embrace life, to accept my past and just say 'yes' to it. Not to let the future haunt me, but to be in the moment, aware of the miracle, which is life itself, which would not exist if death was not one of its hinges."*

Events occur during this period for which we have no real explanation, but which seem to point to other influences actively manifesting themselves. Anyone who has worked in this field will attest to occurrences experienced by the dying patient which had profound effects on them. These paranormal episodes have been extensively researched by several people, including Dr. Raymond Moody, MD who has written extensively on the subject. In my own experience dealing with terminally ill patients I have encountered many such incidents when my patients will report encounters which have profoundly affected them. These have ranged from visitations from deceased family members to strange phenomena like brilliant lights, or Holy people, including Jesus or Mary. These have invariably left the patient peaceful, calmer and more accepting and have served to reassure the family. While it would be easy to ascribe these events to subjective or hallucinatory causes resulting from the disturbed mind. I prefer to think of them as yet another example of the involvement of a higher power. In this context, I will never forget the experiences of my own brother whose life after surgery was a living hell for him, his loved ones and his physicians. All of this changed dramatically after *"he received a visit from Jesus and a discussion they had together."*

Too often we allow feelings of anger, petty rivalry, suspicion or revenge to cloud our thinking and prevent us from sharing and expressing our true feelings at this important time. This is a real shame, for by doing this we cheat ourselves and the patient, and set in motion negative feelings which stay with us long after the event. This is wrong. Instead we should strive to correct these feelings and remove these obstacles and make every effort to come to terms. So that as the journey ends, so would our bitterness. In the end, if we really believe in the continuity of life, we must agree with the words of the great Irish poet and author, *Arthur Joyce Cary* when he wrote:

> *"Look at life as a gift from God.*
> *Now he wants it back, I have no right to complain."*

Conclusion

Sogyal Rinpoche, the world-renowned Tibetan Lama and Buddhist teacher, in his highly acclaimed publication entitled *"The Tibetan Book of Living and Dying",* simply and effectively describes that area of vague and indescribable uncertainty through which we all travel, in one way or another, as we journey on that final road:

> *"…when we finally know we are dying, and all other sentient beings are*
> *dying with us, we start to have a burning, almost heartbreaking sense*
> *of the fragility and preciousness of each moment and each being, and*
> *from this can grow a deep, clear, limitless compassion for all beings."*

Whenever I think of this subject, I am always reminded of a time, many years ago when as a young, relatively inexperienced physician I shared a particularly harrowing and anxious period with a very close friend and relative. He had been diagnosed with a very serious, often fatal septic condition and there was some doubt about survival. When he was subsequently asked to recall how he felt during that very difficult and frightening experience, he described a series of stages which to me were almost identical to *The Five Stages of Grief* so beautifully explained by great Swiss-born, American Psychiatrist Dr. Elizabeth Kubler-Ross in 1969. Even today, so many years after that fateful event, his recollection has not changed in any way, and he still vividly describes the stages through which he traveled during that period. He remembers his initial response of DENIAL and his questioning of the physicians' findings, followed by the feelings of ANGER he felt at life and at God, and his asking over and over, *"Why me, Why me?"*. This stage then progressed to one of trying to BARGAIN with God; *"Give me a break, Lord, I promise I will be devoted to you!"* And when things got worse and the end was beginning to look inevitable, he became DEPRESSED. He felt hopelessly overwhelmed with sorrow and self-pity for being cheated by life and increasingly withdrawn from his family. But then for some reason which he still cannot explain or understand, he slowly became aware of a sense of calm and peace within him as he ACCEPTED the reality of his situation, and tried to make the best of his remaining days, and even began to "look forward" to the end.

This episode and innumerable other episodes I encountered while I practiced my art over a period of more than half a century under varying conditions and in multiple settings, have helped me to more clearly understand and to appreciate the actions of people as they travel on their final journey. They have also served the very important purpose of teaching me that the act of dying is not a random, unrelated event that takes place at the end of a person's lifeline and should best be ignored or avoided as much as possible until it becomes inevitable. Rather, we should make every effort to recognize that *life is but a journey of transition on the map of our destiny, and death is but a continuum of that journey.*

The great Italian Renaissance painter and intellectual genius, *Leonardo da Vinci,* more accurately wrote on the subject of life and death that:

> *"While I thought that I was learning how to live,*
> *I have been learning how to die"*

This statement, though initially appearing to be paradoxical, in fact contains a fundamental truth which we should not hesitate to unconditionally accept. The Buddhist view is even more direct that:

> "*We begin to die from the moment we are born and from that moment we should be preparing for the final event.*"

Unfortunately few societies allow for this truth, and in fact, tend to encourage the very opposite, that life should be lived as if it has no end. We give lip service to the inevitability of death, but live our lives as if this fact does not apply to our living. It is no surprise that when the time comes we are so deeply consumed with regrets that we lose the ability to accept the moment of truth. Far too often, those of us who are in a position to help the patient during this period are tempted to hold back on providing the appropriate information and guidance, treating it as an inconvenient truth, for fear of upsetting the patient or the family. Rather, we choose the safer path of being non-committal and hope that we can get by without being challenged. By doing this we are contributing to the unnecessary suffering and long term pain which lingers on long after the loved one has passed on.

Yet the real truth is that in the end we must all anticipate the inevitability of death as an integral part of living and as such we must, as we must do in every other aspect of living, make preparations for its arrival. The most powerful reminder of this fact is contained in a simple statement in the Holy Gospel, in *The Book of Ecclesiastes, Chapter 3, Verse 1:*

> "*For everything there is a season,*
> *and a time for every matter under heaven:*
> *a time to be born, and a time to die.*"

Irrespective of your belief system, one fact is constant and predictable, and that is, as my nephew is fond of reminding me:

> *"Sooner or later we will all be entering the departure lounge,*
> *And wait for our names to be called."*

Humans, unlike all other members of the Animal Kingdom, find it difficult to accept and adapt to the reality of dying and as a result experience greater pain and suffering. The animal, whether it is the mighty Lion or the humble Otter, will pause to acknowledge the loss and then continue along their way. Humans, by and large, are so preoccupied with the pleasures of living and personal self-gratification, that they either ignore or suppress the reality that death cannot be avoided or worse, believe that they can somehow fool it. There should be no surprise therefore, that most of us arrive on that final journey packed with so many regrets that we lose the real impact of that experience until the final moment of acceptance.

In 2009, an Australian nurse, *Bronnie Ware,* published a brief internet essay based on her 10 year experience as a Hospice nurse entitled *"The Top Regrets of the Dying,"* in which she recorded the five most common regrets expressed by her patients as they approached death. This was so well received that two years later she expanded her presentation by publishing a book under the same title. In a simple, very personal way, she identified the most common regrets expressed by her patients and their need and desire to have them addressed before the final event occurs. She also reminded us that it was possible to avoid these unfortunate situations and die with peace of mind and dignity, if we took care to make the right choices during our lifetime. She further reinforced the truth, which anyone working in the field will readily confirm, that even in dying it was possible to achieve peace and acceptance, as she noted in her essay:

> *"I learnt never to underestimate someone's capacity for growth. Some changes were phenomenal. Each experienced a variety of emotions, as expected, denial, fear, anger, remorse, more denial and eventually acceptance. Every single patient found their peace before they departed though, every one of them."*

In my own personal life, I have witnessed the peace of mind and calm that comes from the acceptance of the inevitable, and the subsequent joy and celebration of the life of the departed which followed. And above all, I have appreciated the good memories that remain long after. Along the way, I have also witnessed the overnight metamorphosis that take place in a few instances where an angry, aggressive, antagonistic patient was transformed into a peaceful, caring and accepting person, which he suggested resulted from a "spiritual" visit. But I have also shared the excruciating pain and torment of one who could not and would not accept the truth and who fought to the very end, cursing his lot, his luck, his life and his God. That pain lingers on forever, and I and the family are robbed of all the good memories of his life that could have been, but were buried by the resentment.

It is clear to me that quite unlike most of the Eastern societies where dying is considered to be an integral part of life; the Western attitude is one of denial and ignoring its relevance in favor of living at all cost. You begin to wonder which of these views is really the more "civilized" culturally. There is a growing tendency in this modern society where so much amazing and wonderful discoveries are being made on a daily basis, and where there appears to be increasing optimism that we will be able to replace and restore destroyed and dying organs at will, that perhaps ultimately we will be able cheat death itself. The most extreme form of this thinking is the increasing interest in the concept of *Cryonics* where the body is preserved in extremely cold temperatures until such time as science catches up with the ability to restore life. While I endorse and welcome all the scientific advancements that have occurred and encourage aggressive research designed to improve the quality of life, I fear that we might find ourselves further lulled into a sense of security that death is indeed not inevitable and that it could be avoided. Already we increasingly cover up the signs of aging with cosmetics and surgery, and we have no hesitation to reverse some of nature's fundamental changes with the ambitious use of powerful hormones in a concerted attempt to stay young. All of this however will serve only to prolong the journey, but not change the outcome. We must never lose sight of this fact, nor should we ever abandon our responsibility to prepare ourselves and those around us to the inevitability of our destiny in God's ultimate plan.

Oh Death where is thy sting; Oh grave where is your victory?
......1Corinthians 55

There is a dignity in dying that doctors should not dare to deny.
........Author Unknown

For death begins with Life's first breath.
And Life begins at the touch of death.
......John Oxenham

Life is not lost by dying; Life is lost minute by minute,
Day by dragging day, in all the thousand small uncaring ways.
.... Stephen Benet

The art of living well and the art of dying well are one.
.......Epicurus

Do not seek death, it will find you. But seek the road which
makes death a fulfillment.
.... Dag Hammarskjöld

If we have been pleased with life, we should not be displeased with
death, since it comes from the hand of the same master.
........Michelangelo

When you were born, you cried and the world rejoiced.
Live your life so that when you die, the world cries and you rejoice.
......Cherokee Proverb

Life is a great sunrise. I do not see why death
should not be an even greater one.
......Vladimir Nobokov

Death like Love is patient.
-Though it is rarely kind and never proud.
.....Christopher Sabga

Approaching the Final Journey

"Don't bother to make any plans,
You are already in the departure lounge
just waiting for your flight to be called"

The above statement was made in jest by my nephew in a different context. But it has always served to remind me that there will come a time in our lives when each one of us will have to face the reality that we have indeed entered the *"departure lounge"* and will be waiting to be called home. How we actually embark on this journey is, at best, unpredictable.

Over my more than 50 years practicing Medicine I have had, as you will expect, the great privilege of meeting and treating a large number of people. Many of these I was able to help, some of them I could not help, and yet there were others who, despite all my efforts, I was disappointed at the outcome since I felt I could have done more. But from all of them, on every occasion, the experience has enabled me to learn something useful and to change a little.

Nothing however, has been so life-changing to me and so rewarding in a special way, as those times when I witnessed the emotional and physical changes undergone by some of my patients as they faced and dealt with catastrophic and overwhelming news about themselves or their loved ones. Even after my many years of experience, I was never able to predict how they would choose to spend the remaining portion of their lives as they traveled the final journey, and equally important, to predict the reaction of the caregivers who willingly or otherwise, were called upon to participate.

Like the great majority of medical students, no one really took time to teach me the delicate art of caring for death and dying. As a result I became very good at diagnosing and treating my patients' illnesses, but very uncomfortable when called upon to deal with the end-stages of life. It took multiple encounters, much trial and error, and repeated reference to the works of such pioneers as *Elisabeth Kübler-Ross* and *Professor Balfour Blount*, who have contributed so much to the understanding of this difficult and unpredictable period. Through their work and those of others, we are beginning to understand not only the stages of fear, grief and uncertainty experienced by the patient and family members, but more important, the significant role of the caregiver and family in the facilitation and relief of symptoms.

Even when forewarned, the final diagnosis of a terminal illness is always devastating news, both for patients and their family. Suddenly, the world is turned upside-down and like no other time before, there is need for reliable information and honest, realistic predictions. In the past, both physicians and family were encouraged to withhold the truth from the patient, assuming that doing so will remove the will to "fight". Now we realize this is misguided and counter-productive, since it served only to build a chasm between the patient and the loved ones and prevent any meaningful sharing and reconciliation.

In 2000, the Public Broadcasting System produced a 4-part series entitled *"On our Own Terms"* narrated by *Bill Moyers*, the accomplished and acclaimed journalist. It dealt in great detail with the emotional, spiritual and economic turmoil associated with terminal illness and explored the various movements towards improving the attitude to, and the care of the terminal patient. It examined, through interviews, the intimate experiences of patients, family, spiritual advisers and caregivers as they struggled through the turmoil of dealing with terminal disease. It examined in great detail the concepts of palliative care, hospice, home care and other end-of-life choices including physician-assisted suicide. It dealt with the legal and other barriers existing as well as the attempts to introduce the relevant changes. But above all, it reminded us of our need to find a balance between *"Heroic treatment and Humane care"*, as well as between *"Dying and Dying with Dignity."* It is a series well worth seeing over and over!

There is no question that every one of us will be making that final journey and therefore it is incumbent upon each one of us to initiate our own preparations. There is nothing wrong in expressing your wishes such as creating *An Advanced Directive,* securing *a Last Will and Testament,* or recording *specific instructions* to special people. I try to use every opportunity to encourage my family, friends and patients to initiate general discussions on the subject as early and as often as possible. For it is only by talking, or better still, recording your ideas and your wishes as well as your hopes and dreams, can your family be guided in the correct direction and be provided with a sense of peace and comfort. We make a serious mistake by only beginning to think about this after we have received the "final word". It should really be started and continued as early as possible and discussions maintained at regular periods.

Some of the best moments I have witnessed in my personal life and professional career have occurred with those people who have succeeded in coming to terms with themselves, their dying and their relationship with God, and have willingly surrendered. These people, instead of experiencing the intense feelings of anger, fear, regret and all the other negative feelings associated with loss and uncertainty, are able to spend the time available in resolving conflicts, cementing relationships and leaving a legacy of peace and love. Not only is the day to day trauma usually felt by the family and caregiver reduced, but the subsequent period of loss and mourning is significantly improved and above all, the deceased will leave with a lasting memory more pleasant and more worthy of them and there life's work.

> *.....This after all, is the best legacy they can leave behind, as they board their final flight home!*

> *The day which we fear as our last, is but the birthday of eternity.*
> *.......Seneca*

> *At the end of life we will not be judged by how many diplomas we have received, or how much money we have made, or how many great things we have done. We will be judged by:*

"I was hungry, and you gave me something to eat,
I was naked and you clothed me.
I was homeless, and you took me in."
......Mother Teresa of Kolkata

God pours life into death and death into life,
without a drop being spilled.
.......Author Unknown

Watching a peaceful death of a human being reminds us of a falling
star. One of a million lights in a vast sky that flares up for a brief moment, only to disappear into the endless night forever.
........Elisabeth Kübler-Ross

We cannot banish dangers, but we can banish fears.
We must not demean life by standing in awe of death.
.......David Sarnoff

Life and Remembering Kind Deeds

The following story, in one form or another, has been around for many years and has been read by millions of people worldwide. The original author is unknown, but the message is clear. It has never failed to touch me with its power of its message and to remind me of the truth of that wonderful quotation by another anonymous author, which is still one of the most repeated statements in any language: "We will not be remembered by our words; But by our kind deeds."

It is being reproduced entirely in the original form in which I received it. I hope that others will have the opportunity to derive as much pleasure and satisfaction as I have obtained, and perhaps learn, as I did, the true meaning of simple human kindness:

During the waning years of the depression in a small south eastern Idaho community, I used to stop by Mr. Miller's roadside stand for farm-fresh produce as the season made it available. Food and money were still extremely scarce and bartering was used, extensively.

One particular day Mr. Miller was bagging some early potatoes for me. I noticed a small boy, delicate of bone and feature, ragged but clean, hungrily appraising a basket of freshly picked green peas. I paid for my potatoes but was also drawn to the display of fresh green peas. I am a pushover for creamed peas and new potatoes. Pondering the peas, I couldn't help overhearing the conversation between Mr. Miller and the ragged boy next to me.

"Hello Barry, how are you today?"
"H'lo, Mr. Miller. Fine, thank ya Jus' admirin' them peas ......sure look good."

276

"They are good, Barry. How's your Ma?"

"Fine. Gittin' stronger alla' time."

"Good. Anything I can help you with?"

"No, Sir. Jus' admirin' them peas."

"Would you like to take some home?"

"No, Sir. Got nuthin' to pay for 'em with."

"Well, what have you to trade me for some of those peas?"

"All I got's my prize marble here."

"Is that right? Let me see it."

"Here 'tis. She's a dandy."

"I can see that. Hmmmm, only thing is this one is blue and I sort of go for red. Do you have a red one like this at home?"

"Not 'zackley .....but, almost."

"Tell you what. Take this sack of peas home with you and next trip this way let me look at that red marble."

"Sure will. Thanks, Mr. Miller."

Mrs. Miller, who had been standing nearby, came over to help me. With a smile she said: *"There are two other boys like him in our community. All three's families are in very poor circumstances. Jim just loved to bargain with them for peas, apples, tomatoes or whatever they needed. When they came back with their red marbles, and they always do, he decides he doesn't like red after all and he sends them home with a bag of produce for a green marble or an orange one, perhaps."*

-I left the stand, smiling to myself, impressed with this man.

A short time later I moved to Utah but I never forgot the story of this man, the boys and their bartering. Several years went by each more rapid than the previous one. Just recently I had occasion to visit some old friends in that Idaho community and while I was there learned that Mr. Miller had just died.

They were having his viewing that evening and knowing my friends wanted to go, I agreed to accompany them. Upon our arrival at the mortuary we fell into line to meet the relatives of the deceased and to offer whatever words of comfort we could.

Ahead of us in line were three young men. One was in an army uniform and the other two wore nice haircuts, dark suits and white shirts ...very professional looking. They approached Mrs. Miller, standing smiling and composed, by her husband's casket. Each of the young men hugged her, kissed her on the cheek, spoke briefly with her and moved on to the casket. Her misty light blue eyes followed them as, one by one; each young man stopped briefly and placed his own warm hand over the cold pale hand in the casket. Each left the mortuary, awkwardly, wiping his eyes.

Our turn came to meet Mrs. Miller. I told her who I was and mentioned the story she had told me about the marbles. Eyes glistening she took my hand and led me to the casket.

> *"Those three young men, that just left, were the boys I told you about. They just told me how they appreciated the things Jim 'traded' them. Now, at last, when Jim could not change his mind about color or size... they came to pay their debt. We've never had a great deal of the wealth of this world, but, right now, Jim would consider himself the richest man in Idaho."*

With loving gentleness she lifted the lifeless fingers of her deceased husband ---*Resting underneath were three, magnificently shiny, red marbles.*

The Final Farewell

*R*ecently while celebrating mass in the Vatican, Pope Francis, the current pontiff of the Roman Catholic Church offered the following profound advice:

> *"Everyone would do well to reflect on their " final farewell" from earthly life and on whether they are prepared to entrust themselves and all they will leave behind to God".*

This statement to me is a powerful endorsement of the need of us all to recognize that we are all travelling along that road and sooner or later we will be called upon to deal with our final farewell. How we approach this will determine, to a substantial extent, how we spend those final moments as well as determine the memories we leave behind.

One of the major neglects we as a society are guilty of is our failure of, or reluctance to, include this aspect of living in our core curriculum of teaching our children. In fact we believe that everything should be done to shield our children and ourselves from having to deal with this painful part of life. We fail to realize that children who are unprepared experience intense feelings of guilt, anger, confusion and animosity to other adults and even to God whenever someone close to them dies. They do not understand that death is as inevitable as living.

Since we tend to carry these feelings of insecurity into adulthood, we should therefore not be surprised that so many adults are reluctant to speak of, far less consider the final farewell. In my practice this was one of my major problems in preparing the family for the inevitable. In most cases I encountered intense denial and resistance whenever the subject was raised and a serious desire to brush it aside with such remarks as *"this is not the time."* This is very unfortunate because so much goodwill and good memories are lost because the family and or the patient were unable to overcome this barrier and to deal with the inevitable.

The truth is that, when the time comes, patients generally appear to have an unconscious and uncanny sense that they are near the end. How they deal with that situation is directly related to their basic attitude toward the end. The more they are prepared and the more they are receptive, the better and more accepting will the attitude be. Unfortunately for the majority who are not prepared, there develops a sense of anger and resentment leading to lasting bad memories involving all concerned.

In my own life, over the years I have shared very close and moving experiences in a number of occasions which left me with a sense relief and gratitude after. The imprint of these moments will last with me to the end. So also is the joy I feel for having been given the opportunity to share them during these particularly difficult times.

-I remember the moment when my late brother who up to that point had become extremely difficult, angry and resentful because of the gravity of his illness. He just was not willing to accept his impending demise. All this changed dramatically after undergoing a transformation follow what he described as a "special visit". As a result of this, there was a dramatic change in his attitude from one of extreme anger and disappointment to one of more acceptance and humility. He spent the last month happily surrounded by his whole family and was able to share his heart and his hopes with all. What could have been lasting pain became happy memories.

-Then there was my cousin Fred who upon being diagnosed with Terminal Cancer chose, rather than staying at home and be sorry for himself, to visit all his friends and family and personally wish them farewell. I shall forever remember the Sunday morning he came to visit me. We had not seen each other for over 20 years yet the warmth and love that existed will remain with me forever.

-Finally, just few months ago a good friend, Jack, whom I had not seen for about 2 years after he moved out of town decided on returning to visit all his old friends. He had been ailing for some time and insisted on making the trip over the concern of his wife and the reluctance of his physicians. Less than 2 months later he passed away. His wife confirmed that after the trip he was a different person, -and so am I!

These are but 3 examples of so many others that I have experienced as I travelled along the road of life. In each of the cases I witnessed the joy and peace and humility that came from acceptance and submission to the final journey. I have also relished the happy memories that remain with all of us who have been left back.

But I have also witnessed the anger and the resentment and the fear in the eyes of others who have not accepted the inevitability of their demise. They become so consumed with disappointment and lash out at everything from their bad luck, to their family and friends, their physicians and even to the Almighty. So much so that what should be a time of sharing, understanding and acceptance becomes sheer agony for all concerned. In the end instead of kind and happy memories we are all left with pain, regret and disappointment. Unfortunately these feelings will stay on even with the passage of time.

As I see it, the only way available to guard against this situation is to follow the advice of the Pontiff as outlined above. We owe it to ourselves, our families and our entire communities to make every effort, by teaching and by example, to spread the word that that we must prepare ourselves for dying as we do for every other aspect of life. We need to truly recognize that, as I have stated previously, *life is an exquisite and precious expression of a greater plan by a Supreme Being in which our time spent on earth is but a short segment of a journey which began in eternity and will continue into eternity.*

If we truly believed this, then it should not be difficult to accept that in order to complete the continuum, life as we know it begins at a precise point and must end at another. We must believe that the journey must continue on to meet our maker. I sincerely hope that when my time comes along, I shall be ready and willing to accept it in peace and humility.

-------*Without this belief, we are lost!*

Oh Death where is thy sting; Oh grave where is your victory?
......1Corinthians 55

There is a dignity in dying that doctors should not dare to deny.
........Author Unknown

For death begins with Life's first breath,
And Life begins at the touch of death.
......John Oxenham

Life is not lost by dying. Life is lost minute by minute,
day by day, in all the thousand small uncaring ways.
.... Stephen Benet

The art of living well and the art of dying well are one.
.......Epicurus

If you are not afraid of dying, there is nothing you cannot achieve.
........Lao Tzu

Do not seek death. Death will find you.
But seek the road which makes death a fulfillment.
.... Dag Hammarskjöld

If we have been pleased with life,
we should not be displeased with death,
since it comes from the hand of the same master.
........Michelangelo

When you were born you cried and the world rejoiced.
Live your life so that when you die, the world cries and you rejoice.
......Cherokee Proverb

Life is a great Sunrise.
I do not see why death should not be an even greater one.
......Vladimir Nobokov

Death is not extinguishing the light;
It is putting out the lamp because the dawn has come.
........Rabindranath Tagore

Where have you Gone Holly?

"When an animal dies that has been especially close to someone here,
That pet goes to Rainbow Bridge.
There are meadows and hills for all of our special friends,
So they can run and play together.
There is plenty of food, water and sunshine,
....and our friends are warm and comfortable."

These beautifully written words attracted my attention as I searched for something to say to the heart-broken little girl upon hearing of the abrupt and sad loss of a little creature who answered to the name Holly.

I had met Holly just two weeks earlier when I visited the home. For some strange reason I found her trying to snuggle up to my leg as soon as I sat down. This was quite unusual for me, for although I like pets, I do not usually pay attention to them and to their attempts to draw attention. But this one was different. I am not sure whether it was her intelligent face, or her wide, inquisitive eyes or the way she waited eagerly for my response. Or it could have been perhaps the exquisite *drawing of her face* done by the little girl that sat in a frame on the table in front of me. Whatever the reason, the little puppy left an impression which even now, several weeks after the unfortunate incident, remains.

Having been a physician for more than fifty years, I have had my fair share of dealing with families of people who have passed on and have spent many hours helping them to cope with the loss. Also during my own life, I too, like everyone else, have lost close relatives and friends and have experienced the pain and sadness and regrets that follow the event. You would therefore expect that with that background, I should be able to comfortably deal with any such event. Let me assure you this is far from the truth, and like anyone else, the loss of life carries a painful responsibility.

This is no different with the loss of a favored pet. In my own family, I witnessed the pain and sorrow of my youngest daughter when her lovebird, Kiki, died, the genuine emotional outburst in my wife and son after Boojou's demise and the sadness and regret in the faces of our neighbors after their dog passed on. To each one of them, the loss was indeed genuine and true. Yet in all these cases the skeptic would respond, in good faith and with a genuine intention of reassurance, that all is not lost since the pet could be replaced. They will never understand the outright rejection of this suggestion and the insistence that the loss was irreplaceable. And so it should be, for I can think of nothing else that provides complete, total and unreserved loyalty and love, without any preconceived rules or conditions or expectations as a pet. This indeed is the real definition of a Pet. Their love is unconditional and they will unhesitatingly give their life in defense or service of their masters.

My own personal views were tempered many, many years ago as a young boy after our family watch dog, Bobby, was poisoned by a neighbor whom he constantly prevented from stealing mangoes from our tree. My immediate response was one of anger and of sorrow, but I still remember the advice of Mr. Thomas, an older man and friend of my father, who reminded me that we should be happy for Bobby for having had the opportunity to feel the love and the attention of his masters. A very spiritual man, he believed that pets were placed here by God to teach us what unconditional love really means, and what God expects from us. I remembered thinking that if this was true, then Bobby had indeed done a great job.

In his humble simplicity Mr. Thomas may well have touched on the real purpose of a pet in the lives of people. Perhaps this may indeed be the way that God has chosen to teach us the real meaning of faith and being true Christians. You only have to compare the absolute trust, love and loyalty of the pet against the distrust, aggression and antagonism of its cousin in the wild to be convinced. So in a way we should rejoice when our pet passes on and instead of being sad and depressed, we should take time to thank God for sending it to us to teach us the way to be good children of God.

Perhaps the current Roman Catholic Pontiff, Pope Francis, may well have the answer when he recently suggested:

> *"Perhaps one day we will all see our animals again in the Eternity of Christ. Paradise is open to all God's creatures."*

Surely this is the most reassuring answer any owner can hope to receive.

The Last Taxi Drive

-This is apparently a true story recorded by Kent Nerburn under the heading "And where there is sadness, Joy" in his book published in 1999 entitled, "Make me an instrument of peace"*. It has since gained wide dissemination because of the fundamental message it carried. A message that is even more relevant today than it has been for past generations.-

*I*t was just after 4.00 pm when I arrived at the address and honked the horn. After waiting a few minutes, I walked to the door and knocked... *'Just a minute'*, answered a frail, elderly voice. I could hear something being dragged across the floor.

After a long pause, the door opened. A small woman in her 90's stood before me. She was wearing a print dress and a pillbox hat with a veil pinned on it, like somebody out of a 1940's movie. By her side was a small nylon suitcase. The apartment looked as if no one had lived in it for years. All the furniture was covered with sheets. There were no clocks on the walls, no knickknacks or utensils on the counters. In the corner was a cardboard box filled with photos and glassware.

'Would you carry my bag out to the car?' she said. I took the suitcase to the cab, and then returned to assist the woman. She took my arm and we walked slowly toward the curb.

She kept thanking me for my kindness. *'It's nothing'*, I told her, *'I just try to treat my passengers the way I would want my mother treated'*.

'Oh, you're such a good boy', she said. When we got in the cab, she gave me an address and then asked, *'Could you please drive through downtown?'* *'It's not the*

shortest way,' I answered quickly. *'Oh, I don't mind,'* she said, *'I'm in no hurry, I'm on my way to a hospice'.*

I looked in the rear-view mirror. Her eyes were glistening. *'I don't have any family left,'* she continued in a soft voice, *'The doctor says I don't have very long.'*

I quietly reached over and shut off the meter and asked her, *'What route would you like me to take?'*

For the next two hours, we drove through the city. She showed me the building where she had once worked as an elevator operator. We drove through the neighborhood where she and her husband had lived when they were newly-weds. She had me pull up in front of a furniture warehouse that had once been a ballroom where she had gone dancing with him, as a girl. Sometimes she'd ask me to slow in front of a particular building or corner, and she would sit staring into the darkness, saying nothing.

As the first hint of the sun creasing the horizon appeared, she suddenly said, *'I'm tired. Let's go now'.* We drove in silence to the address she had given me. It was a low building, like a small convalescent home, with a driveway that passed under a portico. Two orderlies came out to the cab as soon as we pulled up. They were solicitous and intent, watching her every move. They must have been expecting her. I opened the trunk and took the small suitcase to the door. The woman was already seated in a wheelchair. *'How much do I owe you?'* she asked, reaching into her purse. *'Nothing,'* I said. *'You have to make a living,'* she answered. *'There are other passengers,'* I responded.

Almost without thinking, I bent and gave her a hug. She held onto me tightly. *'You gave an old woman a little moment of joy,'* she said. *'Thank you.'* I squeezed her hand, and then walked into the dimming evening light. Behind me, a door shut; ....*It was the sound of the closing of a life.*

I didn't pick up any more passengers that shift. I drove aimlessly lost in thought, for the rest of that day. I could hardly talk. What if that woman had gotten an angry driver, or one who was impatient to end his shift, or what if I had refused to take the run, or had honked once then driven away! On review, I don't think that I have ever done anything more important in my life.

We're conditioned to expect that our lives revolve around great moments which come to us in beautiful packages. But sometimes even greater moments very often catch us unaware, and come wrapped in what others may consider a nuisance package.

> PEOPLE MAY NOT REMEMBER EXACTLY WHAT YOU DID, OR WHAT YOU SAID, BUT THEY WILL ALWAYS REMEMBER HOW YOU MADE THEM FEEL.

..........This story is excerpted from the original which can be found at: *http://www.snopes.com/glurge/cabride.asp*

The Last Journey
A Short Story of Reaching the End

*I*t was to be the greatest event ever planned for any member of his family and one that will be remembered and passed on for generations to come. The Sixtieth wedding anniversary of this great man was due on Saturday August 3rd and for the past year plans were laid to honor him and his wife in a function that was worthy of him and his life.

Plans were laid to facilitate the gathering for the occasion of any and everyone who was directly or indirectly related. These included all his children, his grandchildren, great grandchildren, nephews, nieces and an assortment of family members. They traveled from all over the world, including United States, Canada, France, Lebanon, Syria, Venezuela and Islands of the West Indies.

They began arriving on the Monday and Tuesday of that week. He greeted each one with such love and compassion that many sensed something special and memorable was about to occur.

On Wednesday, he was given an exhaustive medical examination by one of his nephews, who had been his care-giver for the past twenty years and with whom he shared a special relationship. At the end of the examination, he was told that he was in good health and should enjoy this for many more years. He smiled serenely and replied,

"-Saturday, that is all, Saturday."

On Thursday, at a luncheon attended by most of the adults and children of the family, he took time to greet each one present individually. He gave them advice, kissed and blessed each one. He made sure that that everyone knew that he really cared for them and their families. This lasted over five hours and he was involved for every minute of the time.

On Friday, he posed for pictures with his eight daughters and three sons; the photographs of the entire extended family were planned for Sunday morning.

On Saturday morning, he attended a breakfast with the three generations of the male members of the family. He blessed each one and took time to give words of praise and advice.

The evening began with the blessing of the couple by a priest who had known the family for generations. After the blessing, the speeches began.

The first speaker was his eldest son. He spoke with pride and admiration of his parents and their life together. He spoke of the great name and reputation his father had established in the community and of the depth of gratitude he and his siblings owed this great man. He closed by reciting a poem whose author is unknown, which epitomized his father and what he stood for:

> *You got it from your father; it was all he had to give.*
> *So it's yours to use and cherish for as long as you may live.*
> *If you lost the watch he gave you, it can always be replaced;*
> *But a black mark on your name, Can never be erased.*
> *It was clean the day you took it, and a worthy name to bear*
> *When he got it from his father there was no dishonor there*
> *So make sure you guard it wisely after all is said and done;*
> *You'll be glad the name is spotless when you give it to your son*

The next to speak was his grandson. He was the first son of the first son of the great man who was himself the first son of his parents. Although only sixteen, he spoke eloquently of the pride and admiration for his grandparents and how the children were influenced by the example of love, honor and fidelity they have seen from the "Old man".

The last to speak was his nephew, the physician who had previously examined him, and with whom there was a special bond going back many years. He described his life as a journey covering eighty-five years and along the way he spoke of the many milestones which he had left behind, and the impact these have had on the lives of innumerable people. He concluded that his reputation was not only well deserved, but predicted that he will be remembered long after he is called home by his maker.

Then the great man got up to speak. There was a sense of agitation in his demeanor. There was an urgent need to say what he wanted to say. His speech was short and simple. He described his sixty years of marriage to his wife as *"one which had transcended physical Love and had achieved a spiritual level"*. He stressed that his life had been blessed with all the love and happiness he saw and felt around him and thanked everyone for sharing this moment with him. He then turned to the children gathered all around, and addressing them, he said;

> *"My children the best advice I can give are these words taken from the holy bible; Those who please their parents, will please God".*

At this point he paused, closed his eyes and still standing, he died.....

-*No, Not died!* A Man like this does not die, he just moves on. His work on earth was now completed and he had left us to continue his journey onward to meet his God.

> *His nephew was left to contemplate the import of the last words he had heard from this great man a few days earlier and to wonder if in fact, he had known all along. Perhaps one day he will know the answer!*

> *"Saturday, that is all, Saturday, you'll see!"*

Made in the USA
San Bernardino, CA
17 September 2016